HERE COMES DUKE

THE DRIVE FOR FIVE

The Herald-Sun

This book is available in quantity at special discounts for your group or organization. For further information, contact:

Triumph Books LLC
814 North Franklin Street
Chicago, Illinois 60610
Phone: (312) 337-0747
www.triumphbooks.com

Printed in U.S.A.
ISBN: 978-1-62937- 192-4

Duke Athletics and *The Herald-Sun*
Executive editors — Bob Ashley and Jon Jackson
Managing editors — Matt Plizga and Steve Wiseman
Photo/Caption editor — Brad Amersbach
Contributors — Jean Brooks, Art Chase, Cory Foote, Leslie Gaber, Nicole Jones, and John Roth

Content packaged by Mojo Media, Inc.
Joe Funk: Editor
Jason Hinman: Creative Director

Interior Photography Provided by:
Duke Blue Planet
Duke University Photography
The Herald-Sun
USA Basketball

CONTENTS

Foreword *by Quinn Cook*..4

Season in Review 10

The Road to the Final Four 18

Journey Begins with USA Basketball...........................20

Duke vs. Michigan State — Champions Classic 24

Backcourt Chemistry..28

Duke at Wisconsin — ACC/Big Ten Challenge.................30

Cameron Indoor Stadium's 75th Anniversary.................34

Duke at N.C. State..38

Duke vs. Miami...40

Marshall Plumlee 42

Duke, Tyus Try to Rebound at Louisville 44

Duke at Louisville...46

Amile Jefferson...50

Duke at St. John's...52

Duke at Notre Dame 56

Duke's Rough Week...58

Duke at Virginia..60

Duke vs. Notre Dame 64

Justise Winslow...68

Duke vs. North Carolina 72

Duke at North Carolina...76

Road Warriors...80

Eight Is Enough 84

ACC Tournament Quarterfinals vs. N.C. State...................86

ACC Tournament Semifinals vs. Notre Dame....................88

Jahlil Okafor...90

NCAA Tournament Round 2 vs. Robert Morris.................94

NCAA Tournament Round 3 vs. San Diego State.............98

NCAA Tournament Sweet 16 vs. Utah...............................102

NCAA Tournament Elite Eight vs. Gonzaga.....................106

Matt Jones..110

Quinn Cook 112

NCAA Tournament Semifinal vs. Michigan State...........116

NCAA Tournament Championship vs. Wisconsin.........122

Grayson Allen..134

Tyus Jones...138

Homecoming Celebration...142

FOREWORD

By Quinn Cook

It started with some text messages sent at one of the lowest points of my Duke basketball career. We'd just lost to Mercer in the NCAA Tournament in Raleigh in 2014. I didn't want my senior season to end the same way.

So I sent our incoming freshman class — Tyus Jones, Jahlil Okafor, Justise Winslow and Grayson Allen — some texts that day. I was just telling everybody that it starts now. We can't wait until our first practice. We can't wait until we all get here to Durham.

Kentucky and Connecticut played in the national championship game a few weeks later. We all participated in a group chat during the game.

Next year we wanted to be playing in that game ourselves. It would eventually become true, but not before a lot of hard work.

I continued texting the freshmen on a weekly basis, checking up on them. I didn't want to be that annoying upperclassman. I just used my personality, and those guys were drawn to me. I just kept in contact with them. Those guys wanted me to challenge them. I always tried to make sure they were doing what they were supposed to do.

We had a talented team, but I wanted to make sure we were working together toward our goal of being a championship team.

During this time, Coach K and I had an important meeting. My mother was there, too. We talked about my role on the team for the next season, the leadership I needed to provide with my play and actions. All the things that Coach said in the meeting, I felt the same way. It was set in stone. I had to change. I felt I was making the right decisions before that meeting to start my change. My mom was on board. She was supportive.

I decided to spend the entire summer in Durham rather than returning home to D.C. I just wanted to spend every day with Will Stephens, our strength and conditioning coach, to allow him to take my game to the next level. When I'm back home, I'm trying to look for a gym. I had 24/7 access here. I just felt it was a smart decision to stay here.

In late June, the freshmen arrived on campus. We already felt close when they got here. It wasn't like an introduction was needed. Now it was time to get started. That's when the fun began.

We worked as a team on the court and had a lot of fun off the court. We went bowling. We played laser tag. The coaches supervised some of the activities, but we did others on our own.

One Friday, Coach Will surprised us with a Wiffle ball game instead of our normal early morning

Quinn Cook is overcome with emotion following Duke's 68-63 victory over Wisconsin in the national championship game at Lucas Oil Stadium in Indianapolis, Ind. Cook capped off his career having played in 117 Duke victories. (Jon Gardiner/Duke Photography)

workout. Jahlil, Amile Jefferson and Matt Jones organized other things. It just kept everybody loose.

Coach K and Coach Capel were gone most of the summer coaching USA Basketball in Spain. That team won a gold medal at the World Cup of Basketball.

We took something that team did, and it paid off during our run to the championship.

When Coach K got back, he said basically before every meeting, before everything they did, there was a picture of the gold medal on a screen as a reminder of what their goal was. He told us why he did it with the USA team, and he was going to do it with us. All of the trophies we were shooting for the whole year were on the screen. It was our home screen. They were there while coach was talking. We would watch a bunch of film, and then it would be up there again.

We became banner hunters. By winning one of those trophies, either for the ACC regular season championship, the ACC Tournament, reaching the Final Four or winning the national championship, we could hang a new banner in Cameron Indoor Stadium.

At the same time, I didn't want to put too much pressure on the guys. I felt like the banner hunters theme, it was just a goal. Obviously we can't just simulate the whole season to get to where we are winning banners. The regular season was about us building habits and getting better, and I think we did a good job of that. At Duke, we always have the toughest schedule in the country to get us prepared for March.

That schedule sent us to Wisconsin to play the ACC-Big Ten Challenge game in early December.

That was our first true road game. Since I had been here, early in the year, we hadn't performed well on the road. We lost to Ohio State and Temple in previous years. You never know, especially with a younger team with three starters being freshmen in their first road game. Those guys were coming off a Final Four run and had a player of the year candidate, Frank Kaminsky. But our guys, they raised their level. They accepted the challenge. They played fearlessly. I knew we had something special when we won that game.

The next few weeks, though, we didn't build on that win like we should have. You start to feel yourself a little bit. We're No. 2 in the country, we just beat Wisconsin. You start feeling a little bit of invincibility, especially as a young team. You don't really know how quickly things can change.

We didn't practice well. We didn't play well. We took a week off for exams before playing games against Elon, Connecticut, Toledo, Wofford, Boston College and Wake Forest.

Coach K and Coach Capel had been warning us for those six or seven games that we don't want to lose to learn. We need to break these habits. We just kept getting away with it.

That changed Jan. 11 against N.C. State and Jan. 13 at home to Miami. We lost both games.

We went to N.C. State, and all the bad habits bit us in the butt. With the quick turnaround, we felt that we were home and we were going to win against Miami. I don't think we prepared the right way. They got a lead, and we started feeling we had to do it on our own. Guys started making one-on-one moves. We dropped that one, too.

You are the best team, you are being compared to NBA teams on Saturday before you play State and by Wednesday you are a disgrace to Duke. It can go quickly.

Something had to be done. So I called a meeting at my house on Wednesday, the day after the Miami loss. I reminded everyone that it's still a long season.

If we win this next game at Louisville, a top-five team, everybody will start believing in us again. I want everyone in the locker room to still believe.

Coach K had already said he believed in us. After the Miami game in the locker room, he said we are going to go beat Louisville on Saturday. That does a lot as well. We still didn't practice well. But the lights came on, and guys just performed and we won at Louisville.

We played a lot of zone defense that day, something Duke doesn't normally do. It was smart because it caught Louisville off guard. They didn't prepare for zone.

The zone defense did something else — it made us play together more, even when we went back to man-to-man defense. From watching film we saw how active we were together, how much the bigs were talking. Beating Louisville and Pittsburgh brought us close to an important game. If we could beat St. John's on Jan. 25 at Madison Square Garden in New York, Coach K would have 1,000 wins.

When I was a freshman, we gave Coach K his 903rd win to make him the all-time men's Division I leader in coaching wins. Marshall Plumlee was on that team, too. We used that experience to help this year's team with the 1,000th win.

Just like 903, we knew coach was going to get it someday. This wasn't like a fifth championship. We knew he was going to get 1,000 so there didn't need to be any pressure.

Coach made it all about us. He wanted to get win No. 17 on the season. We wanted to get it — and No. 1,000 — for him but also get it for ourselves.

It was like a championship atmosphere. We fell behind by 10 points with eight minutes to go but still won, 77-68. We had the whole world watching. It was a big stage. For us to perform like that on somebody's home court, to come back on a stage like that was tremendous.

That started what turned out to be an emotional week.

Three days later, we played at Notre Dame and lost, 77-73. I felt the team vibe was great going into Notre Dame. They were a top-10 team at the time. I felt we outplayed Notre Dame, but missed free throws killed us. We let it get away, and they made some tough shots, all credit to those guys.

The next day, Coach K dismissed Rasheed Sulaimon from the team. So we're coming off a loss and we had a game at unbeaten No. 2 Virginia coming up in two days.

We've got a player that's going to be missed, and it was back to how it was going into Louisville with nobody giving us a chance. But Coach was telling us eight is enough. He had us believing in each other.

At Virginia, we were behind by 11 points with 11 minutes to play. But we were resilient the whole game. We made that last run and won, 69-63. That was our M.O. all year — never quitting. We couldn't quit when we were down 11. We strung some stops together and played tough. We hit some shots. We beat them, and it felt that eight really was enough. When Coach says something, we all listen. To see it happen, he knows because he is the greatest. He knows every time.

Something else happened during this time that would prove important later.

The week of the N.C. State and Miami losses, freshman guard Grayson Allen hardly played. I told him, "Stay ready, stay ready, stay ready. Stay ready because it's a long season."

I was told that during freshman year and one time, when Coach called upon me, I wasn't ready. I

will regret that for the rest of my life. So I always tell younger guys, like when Amile wasn't playing his freshman year, I always told him to stay ready. When Matt Jones wasn't playing last year, I always told him. Stay ready. Stay ready.

Just before the Virginia game, I went up to Grayson and I said, "Your time is now. We need you."

Less than two weeks after losing that game at Notre Dame, we got another chance to play them at Cameron. We prepared for those guys well. We were mad the whole practice. We were taking it out on the scout team and coaches. We were going hard. We came into that game mad and we played mad the entire game and won, 90-60.

The two games with North Carolina are always the most important games of the regular season. Even compared to the national championship game and the bigger games, there is something different about the Carolina game.

The first game was at Cameron. We got a lead, then Jah hurt his ankle and had to leave the game. We had so much adrenaline going early because it was a Carolina game, but we got tired. Then to see our best player go down, it was a little bit scary. We were playing timid and those guys got it going and took a 10-point lead with four minutes to play.

But my career there are always moments when Coach K just says things, and you just believe it. He said, "We're going to win." That's the difference with this team. Whatever he said, we did it.

Tyus took over, scoring the last nine points of regulation to tie the game. We put some stops together. On the last play of regulation, I got screened, and Matt Jones had the sense of urgency to switch and get Marcus Paige, who missed the shot. We could have lost the game there. We got another stop at the end of overtime and won, 92-90. To get the win, it was

just that belief that Coach instilled in us.

The second Carolina game wasn't as dramatic, but we got it done and won, 84-77, at Chapel Hill. We prepared mad because we were tired of people saying that we got lucky and that we should have lost the first game.

We were still hunting our banners, though. We obviously couldn't win the ACC regular season because Virginia only lost two times, even though we beat them. That was out of our control. We didn't accomplish that one.

At the ACC Tournament, we didn't prepare the right way and lost to Notre Dame in the semifinals. That was pretty tough on us. On the bus, there were a lot of emotions. I cried. Amile was mad. Justise was mad. I remember Jah consoling me, making sure I was OK.

I called the meeting. I didn't want us going back to our dorms, going back to our houses feeling like it was over. I didn't want to carry any negative energy into getting ready for the tournament

I told the guys 'I think we'd rather be national champions than just ACC champions or regular season champions. This is the one that we'll be remembered forever for.' The guys responded.

On Selection Sunday, we were given a No. 1 seed in the NCAA Tournament. We had never had one in my career so that was a pretty big deal. What happened later that night was a big deal, too.

Jah and I regularly got together on Sunday nights to watch our favorite show, *Empire*. We were in the car heading home after the selection show when I said, "Let's go work out." He said alright.

We made a U-turn and went back to the gym. We pull up to the gym, and Amile has Tyus, Justise and Matt in his car. Jah says, "Hey, come inside let's get some shots up or something." We had six players there already. So we just had to track down Marshall and Grayson. We got some shots up and went over plays. That's the type of team we had. Everybody invested in each other. For myself and Jah, really Jah, to call a practice, and I just put my stamp on it.

Nolan Smith was there watching us. He said, "Y'all are special. Y'all are going to do something special in March."

After we did that, it didn't feel forced or anything. I knew we were going to do something special.

We approached the NCAA Tournament like three two-game tournaments. Charlotte was first, where we beat Robert Morris and San Diego State.

San Diego State had one of the best defensive teams in the country. But we took pride in our defense. That's when I felt we really started playing defense at a different level.

Next was Houston, where we had games with Utah and Gonzaga.

Our team is a really laid-back, mellow team, and at these tournaments there is a lot going on. A lot of people partying. There's a party every night in the lobbies. Guys just stayed in their rooms and played video games or they were on the computer. We were with each other all the time.

Justise had a birthday while we were in Houston, his hometown. But he stayed in his room. His family brought everyone food and his family was there when we first got there, but they left him alone. He was in his room the entire time focusing. That's why we won.

We had to beat Gonzaga in the Elite Eight game to reach the Final Four. I know that program is tired of not getting to a Final Four. They wanted to get there, and we knew that. But we wanted to get there, too. The whole tournament, we got better each game with our preparation. It started to become fun. We prepared great for those guys and won to go to the Final Four.

That was an emotional day for me. But it wasn't just because I got a banner; I was happy for everybody. I was so happy because we were just two games away from getting a championship. Just hearing stories from our guys in the program who have been to the championship at the Final Four, it's extremely hard to get there. So to be in the Final Four, it was great. I couldn't hold it in.

Just getting to the Final Four wasn't our goal. So we had another week of great preparation. Guys were excited and we prepared fantastically for Michigan State, who we had beaten earlier in the year.

I knew they were mad. I kept telling our guys, "We beat those guys. You know how we prepare and play when someone beats us." I kept reiterating it to our guys. At the Final Four, you just don't want to be happy to be there. You still have two games left. That's how we felt.

In the national championship game, it was another game with Wisconsin. But it didn't matter. At that point, we could have played earlier in the year and beaten them by 100, and it wouldn't have mattered.

Grayson Allen was ready when he was called upon, making some big plays in the second half and we came back to win, 68-63.

We had done what we had dreamed. I remember me, Tyus and Matt, earlier in March, sitting there in the locker room practicing what we were going to say to Jim Nantz when we were up there after the game for One Shining Moment. We'd all talked about that.

While we were up there, it was like that dream that I'd played over and over again in my head — only it was 10 times better.

#2

ADAPTABILITY KEYS DUKE'S TITLE RUN

By John Roth

Mike Krzyzewski paused just inside the locker room door to absorb the scene unfolding before him, his Blue Devils a boisterous bundle of elation, excitement, emotion. Quinn Cook, their de facto elder statesman, wedged his way into the middle of the black-and-blue, sweat-drenched uniforms and raised his voice to be heard above the celebration.

"Duke is never the underdog," he barked as his teammates clustered even tighter around him. "Hey, look, look — family on three. One, two, three — FAMILY."

Krzyzewski soaked in this unifying moment, the beaming smile of a proud parent enveloping his countenance. The Hall of Fame eyes that had witnessed almost a thousand college basketball victories and countless locker room huddles gleamed with the euphoria of both triumph and togetherness — and what they might portend for the journey ahead. It was a face nobody saw, but a face that visually articulated the thought Krzyzewski would verbally express months later about that night: "We knew getting on the bus to go to the plane that this could be a real special group."

No one would have been shocked if Duke had fallen to Wisconsin on that bone-chilling December night in Madison. The Badgers were an established veteran team, ranked No. 2 in the country and coming off a Final Four season. They featured a dynamic 7-footer in Frank Kaminsky, who would become the consensus national player of the year, and they were hosting the Blue Devils in their rambunctious Kohl Center, where their winning percentage stood on par with Duke's at Cameron Indoor Stadium. Duke was also highly ranked at No. 4 in the polls, obviously talented but considerably less experienced. Krzyzewski was starting three freshmen who were playing in their first true road contest, and his returnees were coming off a season in which they'd fallen to Mercer in their NCAA Tournament opener.

These newly incarnated Blue Devils had

Amile Jefferson (left) and Justise Winslow (right), surrounded by teammates, friends and family, await their NCAA seeding fate on Selection Sunday. Duke learned that it would play as a No. 1 seed for the 13th time in program history later that afternoon. (Raashid Yassin/Duke Blue Planet)

already defeated Michigan State in Indianapolis and had won the Coaches vs. Cancer Classic in Brooklyn, but this was the showcase game of the annual ACC-Big Ten Challenge and a major early barometer for two heavyweights with April aspirations. When Kaminsky drew first blood by quickly burying a pair of three-pointers, the favored home team had made a strong opening statement.

But it was Duke's response that provided an early indication of what might lie ahead. At the first media timeout, barely five minutes after tipoff, Krzyzewski made a significant adjustment to the defensive game plan. The Blue Devils had intended to double-team the post, but after Kaminsky got away from them a couple times early, Coach K bagged that idea and instructed his team to switch on all screens while applying as much ball pressure as possible. Consequently, Kaminsky didn't score for the next 13 minutes, and Duke grabbed the halftime lead, even though its star post man Jahlil Okafor was sidelined with foul trouble.

The Blue Devils continued to play solid defense after intermission, shot a remarkable 71 percent from the floor and turned freshman playmaker Tyus Jones loose on an assortment of high ball screens to secure a noteworthy, confidence-building 10-point victory in hostile territory.

In and of itself, the key defensive adjustment wasn't all that extraordinary; teams frequently tweak their strategy in response to opposing tactics, personnel and the flow of play. But in this case, it served to christen what would become the trademark quality of Krzyzewski's 35th Duke edition — its adaptability. Modification became routine, and change was not only accepted but embraced by an eager, open-minded roster.

"It took a great deal of focus," freshman Justise Winslow said a few weeks after the 35-win campaign

had culminated with a second victory over Wisconsin for the NCAA championship. "We were constantly changing the game plan. In some games we got down and Coach would put something in, want us to do something, and we immediately adapted to it. This team had a great sense of focus throughout the whole season, but especially in tight games when we were down and needed a quick change, or a quick change in the defense to get something done. Our ability to do that really paid off and got us some big-time wins."

Duke's adaptability was most evident on the defensive end of the court, where for three previous decades under Krzyzewski the Blue Devils seemingly owned the copyright on pressure man-to-man. The 2014-15 squad likewise enjoyed sound early-season results utilizing this program staple, its depth and athleticism particularly effective in the full court. But when the team hit a lull in the desultory weeks following the Wisconsin trip, with the collusion of exams and holidays and the start of ACC competition knocking Duke from the ranks of the unbeaten, something needed to change.

Meeting well into the wee hours of the morning following a stunning home loss to Miami — Duke's second straight defeat, and first in three years at Cameron — Krzyzewski and his coaching staff of former Blue Devil captains discussed implementing a zone defense. Nothing could have been further from the realm of possibility than Duke going zone, but by the time the Blue Devils hit the floor four days later at sixth-ranked Louisville, anathema had been assimilated and the 2-3 zone endorsed as an agent of change for perhaps the most important victory of the regular season. The Blue Devils came together to keep the Cardinals' guards out of the paint at a crossroads moment with the direction of the season hanging in the balance.

"We tried to do things constantly that made them talk more so they would get outside themselves,"

The Blue Devils perform in front of the cameras for CBS promotional videos leading up to the national championship game in Indianapolis, Ind. (Jon Gardiner/Duke Photography)

associate head coach Jeff Capel explained. "One of the big reasons for going zone was, (A) our defense at that time wasn't very good and, (B) one of the reasons it wasn't good was guys were worried about individually getting beat. What the zone did was it forced us to talk. It was something we really hadn't done, we hadn't practiced that much, so guys understood we needed each other. We found something there.

"And from there, that's when all the tweaks and adjustments came, all the nuances, all the little wrinkles we'd throw in. That's when those started. And the thing we realized is that our guys loved them. It made them feel more connected. It made them talk more and understand how important each person was out there on the court."

Indeed, from there the defense never rested. Man, zone, zone press, man press — nothing was off the table as Duke evolved into a cohesive, formidable unit during the heart of the season. Down to seven healthy players against Clemson, the Blue Devils unleashed a frenetic 2-2-1 zone press that produced 19 fastbreak points. Against Syracuse in Cameron they enhanced their traditional man-to-man by using Tyus Jones as a "rover" to clog up the lane. For the North Carolina game in Chapel Hill they threw a modified "run-and-jump" element into their press, an ironic twist at the building named for the man who invented that defense, the late Dean Smith. In the ACC Tournament against N.C. State, it was Duke's hybrid matchup zone that thoroughly confounded the Wolfpack guards, rendering the contest virtually over at halftime with the Blue Devils on top 49-22.

One of the more astonishing aspects of the defensive efficacy vs. State — the team that handed Duke its first defeat back in January — was that the Blue Devils didn't install or even practice the defense until their walk-through the morning of the game. Yet they played it to near perfection, adaptability in its finest hour. A similar situation had occurred earlier when Duke visited second-ranked Virginia for a marquee ESPN *College GameDay* showdown. During shoot-around the morning of the game, Coach K introduced a new defense, a 3-2 zone he called "8", that the staff thought might be effective against the Cavaliers' physical wings. With Virginia on top during the second half, Krzyzewski asked the players, "Can you run 8?" They did it effectively for a handful of possessions, took the Cavaliers out of their offensive rhythm and eventually got on track themselves by scoring on 14 of their last 15 possessions to earn a signature win while handing UVa its first defeat of the year.

The Virginia contest was one of several in which the Blue Devils' adaptability enabled them to change the course of a game in midstream. Earlier that week at Madison Square Garden, in the first of three road trips in seven days, they trailed St. John's by 10 late before going on a 15-1 run that led to Coach K's landmark 1,000th career victory. Marshall Plumlee's play off the bench had a major bearing on the rally. At home in the rivalry game with North Carolina, the Devils were down seven in the closing minutes but rode a nine-point flurry by Tyus Jones to tie the game in regulation and then win it in overtime. They also trailed the Tar Heels in the rematch at Chapel Hill, before Matt Jones and Grayson Allen knocked down consecutive threes to put Duke ahead. Forty-four points and flawless free throw shooting from Cook and Tyus Jones made the lead stand, with support from a gritty floor game by Amile Jefferson.

Krzyzewski and his staff kept their fingers on the pulse of this team and also didn't hesitate to veer from standard operating procedure between games when circumstances warranted it. After the roster dwindled to eight scholarship players, the

Head coach Mike Krzyzewski waves to a group of fans following the team's open practice in the lead up to Duke's Final Four contest with Michigan State. (Jon Gardiner/Duke Photography)

duration and intensity of practice sessions had to be adjusted to preserve physical and mental freshness. During the four weeks of postseason, contact practices were virtually eliminated. The new norm became 5-on-0 and team shooting drills, followed by breakouts into individual work. Assistant Jon Scheyer led the perimeter guys and Nate James the posts, their efforts producing distinct individual improvement in several players even as the pressures of the season mounted.

Scheyer, for example, took Winslow through a regimen of shooting and ballhandling drills almost daily, either before or after practice, helping the athletic freshman to not only get past his midseason injuries but to flourish as one of the Blue Devils' most vital performers down the stretch. His February position switch from wing to power forward paid dividends all through March and April.

By the time Duke reached the NCAA Tournament, it had won 29 games and lost only once after January with a starting lineup that rarely changed. What was prone to change was the lineup that made the difference during crunch time. Everyone had their opportunity to shine, so that when the biggest games arrived they were prepared to thrive — with no jealousies over roles or minutes interfering in the family spirit that drove the group dynamic.

Matt Jones stepping up to hit critical threes against Gonzaga in the Elite Eight? That had already happened in a regular-season rout of Notre Dame.

Grayson Allen's spark off the bench at the Final Four? That had already happened at Syracuse, at North Carolina and on Senior Night at Cameron.

Marshall Plumlee and Amile Jefferson anchoring the inside game during the comeback against Wisconsin in Indianapolis? That had already

happened at St. John's and UNC.

Tyus Jones coming through in the climatic clutch? That had been happening all year.

"I think this team took trust to the top level," Krzyzewski said in trying to identify the intrinsic qualities that made his fifth national title team so special and unique. "I'm not sure a team could trust a coaching staff or each other any more than this team. When something new was put in, they looked at it as, 'How are we going to do it?' instead of 'Where do I fit in this? What am *I* supposed to do?' It was more like, '*We're* going to do this.'

"All the things that we did this year, you can call them creative, adaptive, whatever — look, none of those things are going to work unless the group trusts, unless they believe, and that's what these young men did."

Before Duke's NCAA Tournament games, behind closed doors, the words Energy, Effort and Enthusiasm were written on the locker room whiteboard as the headliners of the pregame talking points to the faces nobody saw. Those three E's served the Blue Devils well on their trek through the minefields of March Madness. But when the final buzzer sounded and the confetti fell and the trophy was hoisted into the Lucas Oil Stadium night, it was another trio of E's that enveloped the faces everybody saw. Elation. Excitement. Emotion. Reactions reminiscent of the private family celebration that had confirmed Mike Krzyzewski's vision for his group's potential following the first win over Wisconsin. A win he would label as a defining moment on the court and a defining moment in the locker room.

"And who defined it?" he noted in retrospect. "The players." Adapting, changing and growing closer every step of the way, together in triumph. ■

Co-captain Amile Jefferson holds the 2015 national championship trophy following Duke's 68-63 win over Wisconsin. Jefferson brought down seven rebounds in the game and played stout defense against national player of the year Frank Kaminsky to help lead Duke to its fifth national title. (Jon Gardiner/Duke Photography)

THE ROAD TO THE FINAL FOUR

The Duke University Pep Band brought the feel of Cameron to Lucas Oil Stadium during the Blue Devils' Final Four game against Michigan State and the national championship game against Wisconsin. (Jon Gardiner/Duke Photography)

BLUE DEVILS' FAB FRESHMEN BEGAN JOURNEY WITH USA BASKETBALL

By Steve Wiseman • September 16, 2014

Two years ago, half a world away, Jahlil Okafor, Justise Winslow and Tyus Jones helped win gold for USA Basketball.

While that made the trip to Lithuania successful, it also set the stage for where the three are beginning their college basketball careers.

"The idea definitely started," Okafor said. "Me and Tyus always had the dream of potentially going to the same university together. But in Lithuania, that's where we first mentioned to Justise that it would be pretty cool if he could jump on the bandwagon and go with us."

While Duke head coach Mike Krzyzewski and associate head coach Jeff Capel are in Spain coaching USA Basketball to a meeting against Serbia for the FIBA World Cup championship, freshmen Okafor, Winslow, and Jones are attending classes at Duke. On the court, they're going through workouts with Duke assistant coaches Nate James and Jon Scheyer when not playing pick-up games with their new Blue Devils teammates.

It may not have happened if it wasn't for USA Basketball, which brought the three together on the team that went undefeated in 2012 to win the U-17 World Championship.

"Being overseas in an entire different country, nobody speaks your language, we bonded with all the guys on the team," Okafor said. "But with myself, Tyus and Justise, there was a special connection that we all shared. Having an opportunity to win a gold medal, that's not something everybody gets the opportunity to do. That's something that built our friendship and made it stronger, too."

Lithuania marked a part of their shared international experiences. Jones and Okafor played on 2011 U-16 team that won the FIBA Americas championship in Cancun, Mexico. Okafor and Winslow played with Rasheed Sulaimon, now a Duke junior, on USA Basketball's U-19 team that won the FIBA World Championship in Prague, Czech Republic, last summer.

The belief among Duke's staff is that these experiences will help the three talented freshmen be more prepared to merge with the returning players to help the Blue Devils in their quests for ACC and NCAA championships this season.

"We have an incoming freshman class that really knows each other," Krzyzewski told *The Herald-Sun* earlier this summer. "Three of them have played together on teams that have won gold medals. They

Tyus Jones (left) and Jahlil Okafor (right) were an inseparable pair even before their time at Duke. The duo played alongside one another on the USA U17 team that won the 2012 FIBA U17 World Championship. (USA Basketball)

are ahead of normal freshmen as far as them knowing each other. They won't experience...the loneliness that freshmen will feel at certain times of acclimating to a different environment."

That aspect of the freshman class, which also includes shooting guard Grayson Allen, is more important than ever in college basketball. Freshmen play an even bigger role than ever in the game as players like the 6-11 Okafor, who is projected as the No. 1 pick in the 2015 NBA Draft, impact teams as soon as they get on campus since they'll likely be staying for just one year.

Duke experienced that last season with Jabari Parker, who led the team in scoring and rebounding as a freshman before entering the NBA Draft where Milwaukee took him with the No. 2 overall pick.

The Blue Devils went 26-9, losing to Virginia in the ACC Tournament final, but were upset by Mercer in the NCAA Tournament. Krzyzewski cited a lack of strong internal leadership as a weakness on an otherwise talented team.

This offseason, helping the freshmen assimilate with returning players with starting experience like senior guard Quinn Cook and junior Amile Jefferson is a major focus for Duke.

Having three of the freshman who are already comfortable playing together gives Duke a head start.

"It's given us a better chemistry and camaraderie on the court," said Jones, a point guard. "Playing USA basketball — anytime you are on a USA team, no matter what team it is, they preach team first. It's really all about the team and playing for your country. You have a great bond with the guys on that team, so me, Justise and Jahlil already have a great bond on and off the court. It has made it an easy transition here the first few weeks we've been here."

Back in Lithuania, when Jones and Okafor asked Winslow to consider joining them in college, Winslow initially was hesitant. All three knew it wouldn't be easy for one school to have scholarships for all of them, even though they were three of the best players in the class of 2014.

But the three started putting the word out to schools.

"Some of the schools that were recruiting us but not recruiting Justise, we let them know that we wanted Justise to be on board with us also," Okafor said of he and Jones. "It just worked out that we all ended up at Duke University and we're very happy."

They're very happy and, if things go according to plan, they'll be productive and successful in Duke uniforms this season. They're already taking steps toward that, thanks to helping the U.S. win gold two summers ago.

"Just building chemistry and getting to know them on and off the court," Winslow said. "It really helped with Tyus — getting a feel for the point guard and distributing the ball. Seeing him play, playing with him in practices and games, I know where he likes to pass it to guys. I know where he wants guys to be so I just try to get in those spots.

"Also with Jahlil, playing off of him, feeding him in the post so I can get easier buckets. That sort of thing. Cutting to the basket. The chemistry that we bring together here having played together is great. It's really been helping us in open gym and in practices and workouts."

So while Duke gives to USA Basketball with Krzyzewski and Capel spending the summer with the national team, USA Basketball has in turn helped Duke with Okafor, Winslow and Jones.

"They understand about playing for something bigger than yourself," James said. "It's an opportunity to play for something outside your AAU or high school program. Sometimes guys just don't get it. By those guys being on that stage and playing for something so much bigger, coming here, obviously, playing with Duke on your chest, that's pretty big." ■

Justise Winslow showcased his athleticism during his time with the 2012 FIBA U17 World Championship team. Duke fans were also treated to Winslow's high-flying ability, as his 24 dunks were the second most by any Blue Devil during the 2014-15 season. (USA Basketball)

NOVEMBER 18, 2014 • INDIANAPOLIS, INDIANA
DUKE 81, MICHIGAN STATE 71

A CLASSIC VICTORY

In Okafor's Absence, Tyus Jones Leads Duke Past Sparty

By Steve Wiseman

Duke freshman Jahlil Okafor slumped to the bench with four fouls, and just under nine minutes remained for the No. 4 Blue Devils to hold off No. 19 Michigan State.

What could have been a big problem turned into no problem thanks to another Duke freshman.

Tyus Jones scored 11 points after that key moment, finishing with 17 points, as the Blue Devils beat the Spartans 81-71 in the Champions Classic at Bankers Life Fieldhouse Tuesday night.

Okafor, who scored 17 points, had 15 points when he went to the bench after picking up an offensive foul with 8:58 to play and Duke up 58-51.

Marshall Plumlee replaced him, but it was Tyus Jones, Duke's rookie point guard, who made most of the big plays to help Duke (3-0) extend its lead.

"We all had to come together collectively," Jones said. "We stayed calm and ran our offense. I was able to take what the defense gave me."

Jones hit a layup in transition and, after a

Michigan State miss, sank a 3-pointer and drew a foul. His free throw with 7:58 left lifted Duke's lead to 64-51.

Jones hit another driving layup with 6:08 to play and drew a foul. His free throw gave Duke a 69-56 lead.

By the time Okafor returned with 5:22 left, Duke held a comfortable 71-58 lead. Michigan State (1-1) never drew closer than 10 points again.

Jones' backcourt mate in the starting lineup, senior Quinn Cook, led Duke with 19 points. He liked what he saw from the team overall and Jones in particular when the game got tough.

"When Jah went out with his four fouls, we didn't panic," Cook said. "We came together. Everybody stepped up."

Duke shot 54 percent and committed just eight turnovers. That allowed the Blue Devils to win convincingly despite getting outrebounded 35-25.

"I really thought the play of Quinn, his leadership, throughout the game was big for us," Duke coach Mike Krzyzewski said. "Quinn's

Duke's starting five huddles together during the Blue Devils' early-season matchup with Michigan State. The win required a team effort as four of the five starters scored 15 or more points in the contest. (Mike Bradley/Duke Blue Planet)

presence was really, really big for us. He and Tyus have really developed a great relationship, and then Tyus took off in the second half."

The Blue Devils, who never trailed in the game, pounded the ball inside to Okafor early to build a lead they took to halftime. Duke made its first seven field goals, with Okafor making four of them, as the Blue Devils led 16-9.

Michigan State, although struggling to score on the perimeter, was able to stay in the game due to its strong rebounding. The Spartans had eight offensive rebounds in the first half and gained an 18-11 overall rebounding edge in the first half.

The Spartans cut Duke's lead to 32-29 on a Bryn Forbes 3-pointer from the corner with 4:02 to play in the half.

Foul trouble, though, kept the Spartans from drawing any closer before halftime. Starters Denzel Valentine, Branden Dawson and Marvin Clark all hit the bench with two fouls before the half was up.

Duke freshman Justise Winslow nailed a 3-pointer from in front of the Michigan State bench and, on Duke's next possession, took a pass under the basket and drew a foul. His two free throws gave Duke a 37-29 lead, its largest margin of the first half before taking a 40-33 lead at intermission.

The Blue Devils shot 56 percent in the first half, collecting 10 assists on their 14 made field goals.

Michigan State shot 46.9 percent but made only 2 of 11 3-pointers over the first 20 minutes.

Okafor and Winslow each had 10 points in the first half as did Cook, who made two of Duke's four first-half 3-pointers. ■

Quinn Cook knocks down one of his three 3-pointers against the Spartans. Cook scored a game-high 19 points on 7-of-12 shooting from the field to help guide the Blue Devils past Michigan State, 81-71. (Mike Bradley/Duke Blue Planet)

NOTABLE: With an 81-71 victory over the Spartans, Duke picked up its third win over a five-day span and defeated its first nationally ranked opponent of the season.

JONES AND COOK ANSWER BACKCOURT CHEMISTRY QUESTIONS

By Steve Wiseman • November 20, 2014

One of the situations that jumped out as a potential problem for Duke this season turned out to be a strength in the No. 4 Blue Devils' biggest tests of the young basketball season this week.

Now, with two more games set for the next two days, we'll see if the good times continue.

The chemistry between veteran Quinn Cook and freshman Tyus Jones in the backcourt couldn't have been better when Duke beat Michigan State 81-71 in the Champions Classic at Bankers Life Fieldhouse in Indianapolis on Tuesday.

Cook led Duke with 19 points while Jones scored 17. In addition to the 36 points they combined to produce, the duo dished out 10 assists while playing a total of 67 minutes without committing a turnover.

Cook scored 10 of his points in the first half. Jones had 11 in the second half. Together they were a big reason why Duke (3-0) remains unbeaten heading to a Coaches vs. Cancer Classic semifinal with Temple at the Barclays Center in Brooklyn, New York.

So far, their chemistry is spot on.

"It's been great," Tyus Jones said. "Quinn has helped me along, and I've eased into it. He's a big brother to me on and off the court as I get adjusted to the college game. He'll pull me aside on the court and tell me to look for something different or approach things a different way. At the same time he's giving me confidence and telling me to believe in myself. He knows what I can do out there on the court and he's welcomed me with open arms. It's been really easy to adjust."

Duke coach Mike Krzyzewski couldn't be happier with how Cook has taken hold of the arrangement.

"Quinn's leadership has been off the charts good for us," Krzyzewski said.

Cook said he saw Jones doing things freshmen usually aren't able to do in November. While Jones wasn't scoring much in the first half, he ran the offense and put others in position to score.

That helped Duke build a 40-33 halftime lead.

"I'm proud of Tyus, personally, not just scoring the ball but getting everybody involved in the first half," Cook said. "He took his shot with confidence and he played big for us."

The win over Michigan State came after Duke had dominated two lesser foes in games at Cameron Indoor Stadium last weekend. The Blue Devils beat

The Duke backcourt of Quinn Cook (left) and Tyus Jones (right) helped the Blue Devils rank 13th in the country in assist-to-turnover ratio, combining to record a 3.40:1 ratio during the season. (Jared Lazarus/Duke Photography)

Presbyterian 113-44 and Fairfield 109-59.

Doing what they did against No. 19 Michigan State, though, marked an important step for not only Jones and Cook in the backcourt, but the Blue Devils as a whole.

"You only get confidence through experience, and the harder the situation that you are successful in, the more confidence you get," Krzyzewski said. "Our first two games we were a lot better than those teams. (From the Michigan State win) we should come away feeling really good about ourselves."

Now, the key is to continue the good play with a tough week of travel and trip to New York after a one-day stopover in Durham following the Michigan State game in Indianapolis.

"We've got to turn it around," Krzyzewski said. "That's one thing I like. We have to show maturity in handling things." ∎

DECEMBER 3, 2014 • MADISON, WISCONSIN
DUKE 80, WISCONSIN 70

BADGERING A BIG TEN FOE

Duke Shoots 65 Percent in Victory Against No. 2 Wisconsin

By Steve Wiseman

No. 4 Duke handled its first trip into a road environment just fine with clutch plays up and down its roster Wednesday night.

Four players scored in double figures, led by freshman Tyus Jones' 22 points, as Duke shot 65 percent in a 80-70 win over No. 2 Wisconsin in a battle of unbeaten teams at the Kohl Center.

"We showed a lot of grit," Duke coach Mike Krzyzewski said. "Our defense was good. Our offensive efficiency was good. We had a lot of different lineups out there tonight. Our kids were ready and they never backed down. They showed great composure."

A guard from Apple Valley, Minnesota, Jones played well in his return to the upper Midwest. He scored 14 points in the second half while making four of six shots as Duke (8-0) stayed perfect this season.

"This is everybody's dream to play in an atmosphere like this," Jones said. "This is crazy and very memorable."

Junior Rasheed Sulaimon scored 15 points off the bench while freshman center Jahlil Okafor scored 13 points. Senior guard Quinn Cook had 13 for Duke's balanced attack.

Wisconsin (7-1) was limited to 42 percent shooting.

After Duke led by three points at halftime, Wisconsin hit a pair of 3-pointers early in the second half to pull even. A 3-point play, including a free throw, by Nigel Hayes put the Badgers up 43-42 with 15:10 to play.

But the Badgers wouldn't hit another field goal for nearly five minutes and Duke took advantage to build a six-point lead.

Jones started the spurt by hitting one of two free throws after driving the lane and drawing a foul.

After Duje Dukan missed a jumper for

Tyus Jones sets up an offensive set in what would be the first of two meetings between Duke and Wisconsin. Jones scored a team-high and a season-best (at the time) 22 points to help the Blue Devils earn its first of six wins over a top-10 opponent. (Mike Bradley/Duke Blue Planet)

NOTABLE: Tyus Jones led Duke in scoring with 22 points, shooting 7-of-11 (.636) from the field. Fourteen of Jones' 22 points came in the second half.

Wisconsin, Sulaimon rattled in a 3-pointer for Duke. Jones' driving shot in the lane banked home with 13:47 left putting Duke ahead 48-43.

Frank Kaminsky sank a free throw for Wisconsin, but Sulaimon answered with a runner in the lane to put Duke up 50-44.

Wisconsin's field goal drought ended, momentarily, when Traevon Jackson drilled a jumper at 10:27 to cut Duke's lead to 51-49.

But Duke ran off seven points in a row to extend its lead again.

Justise Winslow hit his first basket of the night, a 3-pointer from the left wing, to start the run. Vitto Brown missed an open jumper, and Okafor banked home a shot in the lane to put Duke up 56-49.

After Nigel Hayes missed a layup, Cook drove the lane to hit a running one-hand bank shot for a 58-49 Duke lead with 8:50 to play.

Wisconsin made its push three minutes later.

Jackson, who scored a game-high 25 points, drilled a 3-pointer cutting Duke's lead to 63-58. Winslow's wild entry pass to Okafor gave the ball back to the Badgers, and Jackson drew Okafor's fourth foul with 5:05 left. Jackson's free throws left Duke up 63-60.

But when it appeared Duke could melt, the Blue Devils came up big again.

Sulaimon sank a jump shot from 14 feet out in the lane for a 65-60 Duke lead. Both teams missed shots before Jefferson sprawled on the floor to tip a loose ball to a teammate and start a Duke fast break. Tyus Jones finished it with a layup for a 67-60 Duke lead.

After Kaminsky missed a shot in the lane, Jefferson was credited with a basket on a goal-

NOTABLE: The Blue Devils shot a season-high 65.2 percent from the field, including 71.4 percent in the second half. Duke connected on 7-of-12 (.583) 3-point field goal attempts, the team's third-highest shooting percentage from behind the arc on the season.

tending call against Kaminsky giving Duke a 69-60 lead with 2:52 remaining.

Duke's hot shooting allowed it to take a 35-32 lead at intermission. The Blue Devils hit 15 of 25 shots (60 percent) over the first 20 minutes, including 5 of 9 on 3-pointers.

Because of that, Duke led most of the first half despite two starters — Cook and Okafor — picking up two fouls.

The game was tied at 26-all as the clock ticked under three minutes to play in the half when Duke hit 3-pointers on three consecutive possessions.

Cook started the onslaught from the left wing. After Jackson answered with a two-point jump shot for Wisconsin, Tyus Jones took advantage of Wisconsin sagging down on Okafor to drill a 3-pointer from the right wing.

After Kaminsky scored inside, Jones hit another 3-pointer from nearly the same spot. Once again, the Badgers decided to double-team Okafor. Jones looked for the big man before opting to shoot himself and give Duke a 35-30 lead with 1:55 left in the half.

Duke had a chance to extend the lead in the half's final minutes, but a pair of Winslow turnovers killed those hopes. ∎

Quinn Cook drives to the basket against Wisconsin's Josh Gasser during the ACC/Big Ten Challenge at the Kohl Center in Madison, Wis. Cook ended the game with an efficient 13 points after shooting 4-of-5 from the floor and 3-of-4 from the free throw line. (Mike Bradley/Duke Blue Planet)

DUKE INDOOR STADIUM OPENED 75 YEARS AGO

By Lewis Bowling • January 6, 2015

This was the thought process behind Duke Indoor Stadium shortly after it opened in 1940. "With the new gymnasium, basketball might make a moderate yield if the people are willing to pay a reasonable admission fee," Duke President William Preston Few said before the first game.

Two days from now, the most famous college basketball arena in the country, Cameron Indoor Stadium, will be exactly 75 years old. It opened on January 6, 1940.

The architectural plans for what was first called Duke Indoor Stadium were drawn by the Philadelphia firm of Horace Trumbauer. The chief designer of Trumbauer's firm was Julian Abele, the first black man to graduate from the prestigious Ecole des Beaux Arts School in Paris. Abele designed Cameron Indoor Stadium and much of the Duke West Campus.

On Oct. 16, 1937, Trumbauer wrote to Duke President William Few, "I am sending you under separate cover rough studies of the proposed indoor stadium designed in accordance with the recommendations I made to you while in Durham this week. The purpose of this indoor stadium would be to provide facilities for:

• Basketball with sittings for 4,000 spectators.
• Indoor tennis which requires more playing space but could be accommodated with sittings for 2,500 spectators.
• Other games of indoor sports in which it is desirable to have seats for spectators.
• Large gatherings such as your commencement exercises with sittings for 5,000 people.

Two days later, Trumbauer wrote Few, "With regard to provision for 8,000 sittings outside of a basketball court, I approximate the cost of the building would be increased to $250,000. For your information Yale has in its new gymnasium a basket ball court with sittings for 1,600. I am quoting this fact as I think the sittings for 8,000 people is rather liberal. The Palestra at the University of Pennsylvania, which is a building used for similar purposes, seats 9,000 and cost $670,000."

A memo on the proposed Indoor Stadium was released on Sept. 24, 1938. Among other items were these: "Under the permanent seats and around the outside of the building would be fitted up for offices for the director of athletics and business manager of athletics, dressing rooms for basketball, two large

Legend has it that Eddie Cameron and Wallace Wade concocted the original outline for the new arena on the back of a matchbook. The project cost $400,000 and took less than a year to complete. (Duke University Archives)

club rooms for the athletic club, dressing rooms for the visiting teams, 10 or 12 sleeping rooms for visiting teams. In addition to this on the first floor will be a hardwood floor of which size, when temporary seats are moved, to have three full sized basketball courts. Directly under the permanent seats will be a concourse extended entirely around the building 12 feet wide for the entrance and exits for the persons seated in the balcony or permanent seats. This building will be located 30 or 40 feet from the present Gym with an underground passage from the dressing rooms of the present Gym to the new building."

So by late 1938 plans were well underway for the construction of Duke Indoor Stadium, sometimes called the Duke University Gymnasium, and eventually Cameron Indoor Stadium. Where the money would come from — Cameron would cost $400,000 — had not been decided. But Wallace Wade's football team of 1938 would take care of that.

The famed Iron Duke team of 1938 went undefeated, untied, and most amazing of all, unscored upon. After the regular season, Duke was invited to play the University of Southern California in the 1939 Rose Bowl. Wade agreed that the money earned from the Rose Bowl would be used to start the construction of the new basketball arena. Proceeds from Duke's win over Alabama in the 1945 Sugar Bowl paid off the debt of the Indoor Stadium, so Duke football pretty much paid for what is now Cameron Indoor Stadium.

Duke Indoor Stadium officially opened Jan. 6, 1940. It was the largest basketball arena south of the Palestra. A crowd of 8,000 was at the time the largest in the history of southern basketball. Add Penfield, longtime radio voice of the Blue Devils, was there. He recalled, "The seats were full. There were a number of dignitaries on hand. Not long after 8:00, the electricity failed, and every light in the building went out for 20 minutes. The only source of light in the place was lit cigarettes in the crowd."

The lights came back on and Duke, coached by Eddie Cameron, beat Princeton 36-27. Tom Connelly missed the first shot of the game for Duke. He recalled years later, "I was tight from nervousness. We had been in the new gym only once before. We went there the night before the game for a workout. Those 8,000 people scared me." Connelly, who later became a jeweler in downtown Durham, did score four points in the game.

Duke Indoor Stadium in 1972 became Cameron Indoor Stadium in honor of Eddie Cameron. In 1977 the original playing floor was replaced, new bleacher seats added, and the lobbies were remodeled. A plan to expand the stadium by 6,000 seats was canceled in 1986 and 1987. Tom Butters, former athletic director at Duke wrote in 1987: "In exchange for 6,000 additional seats, we would sacrifice the intimacy of Cameron Indoor Stadium and perhaps alter forever its unique character. Additionally, the building has as much national acclaim as any arena associated with a university. Wrigley Field is not the Astrodome, but then, does it need be?"

Mike Krzyzewski also agreed with the decision in 1987 to renovate Cameron Indoor Stadium but not to expand. Coach K wrote to Duke fans: "I believe it is important for Duke fans to know that I am very happy with the decision to renovate rather than to expand Cameron Indoor Stadium. It would have been easy for us to get caught up in the recent trend to build ever bigger on-campus basketball facilities. For many schools, that is the right thing to do. For Duke, I think it would have been a mistake ... It is one of the most famous basketball arenas in the country and one of the most feared by opposing teams. Why, then, should we change it? The answer, of course, is that we shouldn't change it." ■

Justise Winslow elevates to throw down an emphatic dunk against Boston College Jan. 3 in front of a sold-out crowd in Cameron Indoor Stadium. The game served as the 75th-year celebration for the venue, which opened its doors Jan. 6, 1940 with a game against Princeton. (Jon Gardiner/Duke Photography)

Significant Dates In Cameron History

- **1/6/1940** — Duke opens play at Duke Indoor Stadium with a 36-27 win over Princeton.

- **2/29/1952** — Dick Groat scores 48 points in his final home appearance to set the single-game scoring record at the venue.

- **2/11/1965** — Duke scores a school record 136 points to defeat Virginia in the final home game of the season.

- **2/27/1997** — Duke defeats Maryland, 81-69, in the 700th game in Cameron Indoor Stadium history, clinching the ACC regular-season title in the process.

- **2/28/1998** — Duke rallies from a 17-point deficit to defeat North Carolina, 77-75, as Coach Krzyzewski earned his 500th career coaching victory.

- **11/17/2005** — Duke dedicates court inside Cameron Indoor Stadium to Coach Krzyzewski after the Blue Devils defeat Villanova, 98-85, to earn Coach Krzyzewski's 500th win at Duke.

Cameron... By The Numbers

- **9-1** — Duke's home record during its first season playing in Cameron Indoor Stadium

- **36-27** — Score of Duke's first win in Cameron Indoor Stadium (vs. Princeton)

- **11** — Undefeated seasons under Mike Krzyzewski

- **832-154** — all-time record at Cameron Indoor Stadium

- **389** — consecutive sellout streak at the close of the 2014-15 season

- **46** — Duke's longest home win streak, which spanned 1997-2000 and leads the ACC

JANUARY 11, 2015 • RALEIGH, NORTH CAROLINA
N.C. STATE 87, DUKE 75

RED-HOT WOLFPACK

N.C. State Hits 10 3-Pointers, Hands Duke its First Loss

By Steve Wiseman

The answers No. 2 Duke offered to every challenge on the court this season were plentiful.

From dead-eye 3-point shooting to slick passing to strong interior play to defensive stops, the Blue Devils had it all.

On Sunday, all of that came crashing down on Duke at PNC Arena.

N.C. State delivered red-hot 3-point shooting combined with solid interior play on both ends of the court.

When it was done, the Wolfpack throttled Duke 87-75 to hand the Blue Devils their first defeat of the season.

N.C. State (12-5, 3-1 in ACC) hit 10 of 16 3-pointers (62.5 percent) and shot 55 percent overall to score more than any team has against Duke all season. Those shooting percentages were season highs against Duke (14-1, 2-1 in ACC) as well.

Before Sunday, no team had shot better than 50 percent overall or 43.8 percent on 3-pointers against the Blue Devils.

"As guards we got caught in screens a little bit too much," said Duke sophomore Matt Jones, who drew his first starting assignment of the season. "They were very hot from 3 starting out. Them being hot from 3 just gave them confidence throughout the game. We couldn't really calm them down."

Behind Trevor Lacey (21 points) and Ralston Turner (16 points), the Wolfpack took a 37-33 halftime lead and pushed it to as large as 19 points in the second half.

It was a strange place for Duke, which before heading on the road in ACC play last Wednesday at Wake Forest had yet to trail in the second half or by more than four points at any time this season.

Duke players admitted the team wasn't tough enough, particularly on defense, to win an ACC road game against a team playing well. Duke coach Mike Krzyzewski concurred, but said it's part of the process for a team that starts three freshmen.

"I don't think we were as tough as we needed to be," Krzyzewski said. "I don't think that means we are bad people or anything. I think you learn through experience how tough you need to be. You might think you are playing tough until you are placed in another situation that requires a whole other level. Were we are tough as we needed to be? No. Does that mean we're soft? No. We're a good team and we need to learn to play at that level. You have to be in these things to learn that."

N.C. State's high-powered offense benefitted greatly from Lacey and Turner, who combined to make 9 of 14 3-pointers. But the Wolfpack showed

Tyus Jones goes up and under the basket at PNC Arena to avoid the outstretched arm of N.C. State's Kyle Washington. (Jon Gardiner/Duke Photography)

a complete offense.

Hulking sophomore BeeJay Anya, all 6-9 and 250 pounds of him, came off the bench to score 14 points, grab six rebounds and block four shots in 19 minutes of play.

"Terrific," Krzyzewski said of Anya. "Unbelievable, terrific performance. That's a hard working kid, big. And he completed plays. That was a huge difference in the game."

N.C. State coach Mark Gottfried has seen his team lose to Wofford and Purdue this season. But the production the Wolfpack got in the inside, from Anya and Kyle Washington (nine points, four blocks) made them a different team.

"We're used to seeing Trevor make big shots and Ralston make big shots," Gottfried said. "But we got some production inside which changes our team. It takes the pressure off our perimeter to score as much. BeeJay, I thought, was just fantastic in there."

Duke freshman center Jahlil Okafor scored 23 points and grabbed 12 rebounds in a productive day. The Blue Devils as a whole, though, struggled to a season-low 36.9 shooting percent while making just 7 of 27 3-pointers.

N.C. State used frequent double-teams to slow down Okafor, whose points came in bursts in the game's opening minutes and then late in the second half. Duke's poor perimeter shooting made it hard to win.

"I think today, including myself and my teammates, we struggled to knock down open shots," Okafor said. "Earlier this season, my teammates were great when I passed out of double teams. When they start hitting shots, it makes it hard for them to double team."

For Gottfried, it was the kind of defensive performance a coach craves.

"I thought our guys defensively locked in," Gottfried said. "We doubled in the post when we needed to. We recovered out of the double teams at times pretty well trying to make things difficult for their shooters and drivers while at the same time trying to take away Okafor's 1-on-1 opportunities which is hard to do." ■

JANUARY 14, 2015 • DURHAM, NORTH CAROLINA
MIAMI 90, DUKE 74

CANES END CAMERON STREAK

Miami Connects on 18 of 27 Second-Half Shots to Rout Duke

By Steve Wiseman

No. 4 Duke appeared invincible for the college basketball season's first two months.

Now even venerable Cameron Indoor Stadium isn't enough to save the reeling Blue Devils.

Duke suffered its second loss in three days as Miami ended the Blue Devils' 41-game home court winning streak with a 90-74 ACC win on Tuesday night.

Coupled with Sunday's 87-75 loss at N.C. State, the Blue Devils (14-2, 2-2 in ACC) are suddenly riding a losing streak after winning their first 14 games.

Duke had not lost back-to-back regular season games since February 2009 when UNC and Boston College beat the Blue Devils in consecutive games.

Counting postseason, it's only the third time in the last six seasons Duke has dropped back-to-back games.

The Blue Devils had also not lost at Cameron Indoor Stadium since March 3, 2012, when UNC beat Duke 88-70.

Miami followed a similar script to how N.C. State handled Duke. The Hurricanes were deadly from behind the 3-point line, making 10 of 20 attempts. Miami hit 6 of 9 in the second half as it made 18 of 27 shots overall over the final 20 minutes to pull away

after Duke led 35-34 at intermission.

"Man they kicked our butts," Duke senior guard Quinn Cook said. "You saw it. The whole world saw it."

Guards Angel Rodriguez (24) and Manu Lecomte (23) paced the Hurricanes (12-4, 2-1). They combined to make 7 of 10 3-point attempts.

They mostly found paths to the lane on dribble drives as Duke showed vulnerability in its perimeter defense once again.

"Our defense has been nonexistent for two games," Krzyzewski said. "I'm not sure if we hit the wall a little bit."

After making just 7 of 27 3-pointers in the loss to N.C. State at PNC Arena on Sunday, Duke struggled there again, too. The Blue Devils hit just 6 of 21 while shooting 43.9 percent overall. Duke made just 43.2 percent of its shots in the second half when Miami pulled away.

The Blue Devils also turned the ball over 15 times.

"We're not as confident as we have been," Krzyzewski said. "I think that's part of being young. We're playing real well and whatever and adversity hits or it's not going as well you start thinking a little too much."

Freshman center Jahlil Okafor had 15 points

Quinn Cook attempts to lay the ball in against Miami's defense that caused 15 Duke turnovers and limited the Blue Devils to 28.6 percent shooting from 3-point range. (Jon Gardiner/Duke Photography)

and 15 rebounds but made just 6 of 13 shots. He also turned the ball over twice.

Fellow freshmen starters Tyus Jones and Justise Winslow each played among their poorest games of the season.

Jones made just 2 of 9 shots, including missing all three 3-pointers, to score six points. He had two assists and two turnovers.

Winslow made 1 of 6 shots, missing both his 3-pointers. He had two points, two rebounds and two turnovers.

Meanwhile, Miami entered Cameron Indoor Stadium with confidence and nothing happened on the court to dampen it.

"The moment we started preparing for Duke," Rodriguez said, "we were talking about the way they play defense and the way we like to play offense. We felt like it was a great matchup and they were going to allow us to do what we want to do."

Rodriguez gave Duke fits in the half-court throughout the first half. The quick guard scored nine points and handed out three assists over the first 20 minutes with his ability to drive past Duke's perimeter defense and into the lane.

On the offensive end, Duke shot poorly from the perimeter, making only 3 of 9 3-pointers in the first half. The Blue Devils shot 44.8 percent overall to lead 35-34 at halftime.

Okafor led Duke with nine points in the first half while Rasheed Sulaimon provided a spark off the bench with eight points. Sulaimon made two of his four 3-pointers while the rest of the Blue Devils made one of five.

Amile Jefferson had a standout first half as well, hitting all four of his field goal attempts to score eight points while grabbing seven rebounds.

But in the second half, everything fell apart for Duke. Down 47-46 after a Cook 3-pointer, Duke saw Miami run off 10 consecutive points to take control of the game for good with 11:46 to play.

Rodriguez and Lecomte had 3-pointers during that stretch that gave the Hurricanes a 57-46 lead.

Duke never drew closer than seven points again.

In the game's final minutes, Miami's lead grew to as large as 20 points. The sold-out Cameron Indoor Stadium fell mostly silent as the final seconds ticked off the clock.

"To hear Cameron like this is not a good feeling," Cook said. "We don't like this feeling. We've just got to get back to that sense of urgency and we'll be fine." ■

40

MARSHALL PLUMLEE

Big Man Aims to Be an Officer and a Blue Devil
By Steve Wiseman • January 23, 2015

With his teammates already in their Duke blue practice uniforms on Friday, Marshall Plumlee dressed in far more formal attire with practice looming at Cameron Indoor Stadium.

A redshirt junior center, basketball was pushed aside, just momentarily, for a ceremony that solidified a life-changing decision.

With Duke captains Quinn Cook and Amile Jefferson holding an American flag as a backdrop, Plumlee wore a formal Army ROTC uniform as he took the oath during his personal Army ROTC contracting ceremony.

He also signed a contract, which admits him to the Advanced Course, a component of cadet command which allows Plumlee to work toward becoming an officer in the United States Army.

"It's a tremendous honor," Plumlee said. "I'm just blessed to have these passions — basketball and the Army — and to be able to pursue both of them. I love basketball. I love Duke basketball and I feel like the Army only makes me a better basketball player. I feel like playing for Coach K and Duke basketball only makes me a better Army officer."

Plumlee has already completed two years in Duke's Army ROTC Basic Course. Members of the Blue Devil Eagle battalion were also present for Friday's ceremony.

Lt. Col. Keirya Langkamp presided over the event.

"This is a pretty historical moment," Langkamp said. "Things like this don't happen very often. It's magical when you get someone of (Plumlee's) caliber, that's part of such an extraordinary team, the Duke basketball team. He's already part of an amazing group of men. Now he's part of something bigger."

Plumlee said he'd always been interested in the Army while growing up. That feeling intensified during his junior year of high school when he traveled with USA Basketball to Germany and met with Gen. Robert Brown.

Plumlee's older brothers, Mason and Miles, were already playing basketball at Duke for Mike Krzyzewski, a West Point graduate and former Army coach. Marshall Plumlee was headed to Duke, too.

Coincidentally, the 6-7 Brown played for Krzyzewski at Army back in the 1970s.

"I told him I had an interest in the military and he pulled me aside and helped me cultivate that," Marshall Plumlee said. "That's a friendship that's grown over the last few years as he has become a two-star and now a three-star general."

Plumlee traveled with Duke director of

Marshall Plumlee follows Lt. Col. Keirya Langkamp's lead during his ROTC contracting ceremony held in Cameron Indoor Stadium. (Raashid Yassin/Duke Blue Planet)

basketball operations Pat Thompson one summer to Fort Benning, Georgia, where Brown was in charge of the troops.

"The combination of him and Coach K and the passion I have on my own has brought me to the point of joining the Army," Plumlee said.

Plumlee's plan is to be an officer in the Army Reserves. He said he'll play his final season at Duke in the 2015-16 season, while attending graduate school, and pursue his dream of joining his older brothers in the NBA as well.

"My dream is to play in the NBA, and that dream is still possible," Plumlee said. "I can still serve as a reserve officer and coordinate with the Army and knock out my service throughout the off-season working hand-in-hand with basketball and the Army. They really complement each other. The Army helps me with the basketball and I feel like the basketball helps me show the Army how much it can open doors."

Plumlee's involvement with ROTC, along with his Duke classes and basketball commitments, means he has to manage his time well. He's proven that's not a problem.

"He really has three very time consuming

areas," Langkamp said. "That's what makes him extraordinary. He's able to create balance with both being a scholar, an athlete and a soldier. That's rare, to be able to have that stamina, intellect and sheer drive to be able to pursue and excel in all three of those areas. He is taking the road less taken. And he's ready for it."

Plumlee's 7-foot stature does preclude him from some assignments, such as riding in tanks or helicopters. The Army approved a waiver allowing him to join.

"There are some things that no matter how bad I want to do them," Plumlee said. "But I know there is some way I can help serve."

His relationship with Krzyzewski, who has continued to support the military throughout his coaching career, has helped everyone be at ease with the situation.

But Plumlee said Krzyzewski's assistance goes deeper than simply opening some doors.

"More importantly, he knows what this means to me as a person having been there himself," Plumlee said. "He has an appreciation for what drives me and he uses that to bring out the best in me." ■

DUKE, TYUS TRY TO REBOUND AT LOUISVILLE

By Steve Wiseman • January 16, 2015

By scoring 15 points or more in six of his first 11 collegiate games, Duke's Tyus Jones had done enough to earn merit as one of the nation's top players.

He's among 25 players on the preseason watch list for the Wooden Award, one of the national player of the year honors.

But, like his suddenly vulnerable Duke Blue Devils, Jones has hit a lull just as ACC play is kicking into high gear.

The freshman guard from Apple Valley, Minnesota, hasn't reached double figures in scoring in his last five games, averaging a meager 5.1 points per game over that stretch.

During No. 4 Duke's last two games, stunning, double-digit losses to unranked N.C. State and Miami, Jones has made just 3 of 15 shots to score 10 total points. He's handed out six assists with four turnovers.

As Duke heads to No. 6 Louisville Saturday for a difficult league game, Jones mirrors his reeling team by looking for answers in a tough venue.

"Shots just aren't falling for me," Jones said. "I have to take them with more confidence. Just play with a clear mindset and try to do my best to help this team win. We'll regroup, get a clear mind and be ready to go."

His shooting slump has coincided with a team-wide downturn in offense.

Duke (14-2, 2-2 in ACC) has shot 36.9 percent and 43.6 percent during the losses to N.C. State and Miami. The Blue Devils have made only 13 of their last 48 3-pointers.

That shows that Jones, who has missed his last six 3-pointers, isn't alone in his struggle.

Duke coach Mike Krzyzewski admitted the team's three freshmen starters, Jahlil Okafor, Justise Winslow and Jones, appear to have hit the proverbial wall that many freshmen have to fight through in their first collegiate season.

"It's a long year, and those three kids haven't been through it," said Krzyzewski, who has 997 career Division I coaching wins.

But Krzyzewski admits the team isn't at the full confidence level needed to compete in a league like the ACC. And, he said, it's not just the freshmen.

"I just don't think we're confident right now," Krzyzewski said. "I'm not saying we have no confidence. Confident when we shoot it, I just don't see it. I don't feel it, and that happens. It can happen to a baseball team with hitting, and I think it can happen with a younger group more than an older group.

"If that had happened to a veteran team, they're going to play harder defensively or rebound and execute. They know if we're not scoring many runs that we better do something, or do something else. That's a part of learning."

After scoring a season-best 20 points in Duke's 73-65 win at Wake Forest on Jan. 7, Winslow slumped during the two-game losing streak. He's made just 4 of his last 19 shots, including 1 of 8 3-pointers.

He even missed all four of his free throws against Miami.

"We're just not as confident as we have been,"

Tyus Jones awaits his introduction, prior to the start of Duke's game against Louisville in Louisville, Ky. Jones contributed 10 points and eight assists, helping to right the ship following Duke's back-to-back losses. (Raashid Yassin/Duke Blue Planet)

Krzyzewski said. "I think that's part of being young."

Okafor, who is also a player of the year candidate included on the Wooden Award's preseason watch list, continues to produce. He's averaging an ACC-best 18.9 points per game and is third in the conference in rebounding at 9.4.

Even with teams increasing their use of double-team defenses against him, Okafor has recorded double-doubles over Duke's last three games. He scored 23 points and grabbed 12 rebounds in the 87-75 loss at N.C. State last Sunday and produced 15 points and 15 rebounds as Miami stopped Duke 90-74 last Tuesday night at Cameron Indoor Stadium.

"Teams are doubling Jah really hard, and he's handling it beautifully," Duke junior forward Amile Jefferson said. "I don't know another player that could come close to handling it how he's handling it.

But we've just got to figure it out, especially on the defensive end, as a team. We've just got to get better from this."

Jones echoed his older teammate and fellow starter. As painful as Duke's first two-game regular-season losing streak since February 2009 has been, it hasn't ruined the Blue Devils' long-term hopes, dreams and goals for this season.

But with road games against ranked foes Louisville, St. John's, Notre Dame and Virginia on the schedule between now and the end of January, Duke has to get better in hostile situations.

"We just have to be better," Jones said. "There are adjustments that we have to make and we are going to make them. It's a learning situation where we are in the season, and we have to come together. I know this group. We'll do that." ∎

JANUARY 17, 2015 • LOUISVILLE, KENTUCKY
DUKE 63, LOUISVILLE 52

ZONED IN

Change in D Halts Two-Game Losing Streak
By Steve Wiseman

Consecutive Duke losses led to strange days in Durham.

Players held meetings on their own, without coaches, to foster togetherness.

Coach Mike Krzyzewski, staunch purveyor of man-to-man defense, told his team to play zone.

It was wacky. It was crazy. But it worked.

The No. 4-ranked Blue Devils, after struggling defensively in losses to N.C. State and Miami, rode a stout zone defense and poor Louisville shooting to beat the No. 6-ranked Cardinals 63-52 Saturday in ACC basketball at the KFC Yum! Center.

"We played together today," Duke freshman center Jahlil Okafor said. "Coaches talked about how we may have taken winning for granted. Today we came together, how we started the season. Five guys playing together as one. That's how we came out with the win."

Duke's first two-game ACC losing streak since February 2009 didn't morph into the Blue Devils' first three-game league losing streak since the 2006-07 season.

Instead, the Blue Devils (15-2, 3-2 in ACC) built a 10-point halftime lead and pushed it to as many as 21 points in the second half as Louisville failed to adjust to a defense normally foreign to Duke.

"We practice zone offense every game, every day," Louisville coach Rick Pitino said. "Do we expect them to play zone? Well, they never did."

According to ESPN research, Duke had only played zone 3.7 percent of the time this season.

But after N.C. State and Miami averaged 88 points while beating the Blue Devils over the previous seven days, Krzyzewski opted for the zone.

The plan worked as No. 6-ranked Louisville (15-3, 3-2) hit just 4 of 25 3-pointers and shot 29.5 percent overall.

The zone didn't prevent Louisville from getting open looks at the basket on the perimeter, Krzyzewski admitted.

"They missed shots," he said. "We were lucky about that."

But it was designed to cut off dribble

Head coach Mike Krzyzewski communicates with his team from the Duke bench. Krzyzewski's willingness to switch from Duke's traditional man-to-man defense to zone allowed the Blue Devils to end a two-game skid. (Raashid Yassin/Duke Blue Planet)

penetration into the lane, which N.C. State and Miami used to carve up the Blue Devils. It also helped Duke contain Louisville star forward Montrezl Harrell, an AP preseason All-American.

Harrell scored 10 points while making just 4 of 10 shots.

"For us it was about protecting the paint playing the zone and I thought we did a really good job in it," Duke junior forward Amile Jefferson said.

Playing well as a group was also a focus for this game, the first time Hall of Fame coaches Krzyzewski and Pitino squared off against each other in league play.

After absorbing an 87-75 loss at N.C. State last Sunday and a 90-74 setback to Miami at Cameron Indoor Stadium on Tuesday night, the Blue Devils searched for answers.

The players held several meetings on their own, trying to recapture the formula that led Duke to win its first 13 games of the season by 10 points or more.

"It brought us together as a team," Okafor said. "We always talk about how close we are and we're one family. We wanted to see how we were going to react when stuff hits the ceiling. We responded well."

The zone itself was one thing. But Krzyzewski felt that Duke's own struggles to make perimeter shots was hurting the team's focus on defense.

So he decided to mix things up and the zone was the thing.

"I think our offense has negatively affected our defense," Krzyzewski said. "Today, giving them something a little different to do, where they had each other's backs, helped them even though we're still not there offensively."

Duke shot 48.8 percent, far better than it did against N.C. State and Miami, but still struggled on the perimeter. The Blue Devils made only 4 of 15

NOTABLE: Duke deviated from its traditional man-to-man defense and played zone defense to some impressive results in a road win over No. 6 Louisville. The Blue Devils limited the Cardinals to 18-of-61 (.295) shooting from the field, the lowest shooting percentage by a Duke opponent all season. Louisville was just 4-of-25 (.160) from beyond the arc after Duke's previous two opponents combined to shoot 20-of-36 (.556) from 3-point range.

3-pointers at Louisville, making them 17 of 63 (27 percent) over the last three games.

Jefferson and Okafor were able to provide the scoring punch. That was enough against offensively-challenged Louisville.

Jefferson scored a game-high 19 points on 6-of-7 shooting. He also made seven of nine free throws. Okafor made eight of his 10 shots and was perfect on his two free throws to score 18 points.

"Jah was really patient," Krzyzewski said. "Louisville is such a good defensive team, tough to score against. All of the sudden things opened up and he goes 8 for 10. I thought it was a really mature performance for the youngster to be able to do that."

The Blue Devils as a whole showed maturity, posting their second win this season on the home court of a top-10 team. Duke also won 80-70 at then No. 2-ranked Wisconsin in December.

"It was just a time that we had to come together," Tyus Jones said. "We had to buy in. We had to play for each other. Really we had to go out there and represent Duke basketball. That's what we did. I'm proud of the guys and how hard we played and how well we executed. Our game plan, we just ran it really well." ∎

The Blue Devils huddle late in the game against Louisville. The team's zone defense played a key role in forcing the Cardinals to shoot just 29.5 percent from the floor and score just 52 points in the game. (Raashid Yassin/Duke Blue Planet)

NOTABLE: Amile Jefferson served as Duke's leading scorer in the game, connecting on 6-of-7 (.857) shot attempts to record a career-high 19 points.

21

FORWARD

AMILE JEFFERSON

When Leadership Is Needed, Team Captain Provides It
By Steve Wiseman • January 18, 2015

One of two team captains for No. 4 Duke this season, Amile Jefferson knew he had to do something.

The Blue Devils had lost consecutive ACC games for the first time since February 2009. A game at No. 6 Louisville loomed next.

"I've been trying to figure out how to lead," Jefferson said. "Those two games I didn't feel like I did a good job. I was talking to guys after the games, but I felt we needed something on the court. I was just trying to bring emotion and energy. That's what the coaches wanted. They wanted us to bring energy, and I just tried to respond to that. Just tried to lead the group."

He brought energy and emotion, along with points and rebounds, to put Duke back in a familiar place.

Jefferson's game-high 19 points were a major reason why the Blue Devils won 63-52 over Louisville at the KFC Yum! Center on Saturday to end their rare losing streak at just two games.

A 6-9 junior forward from Philadelphia, Jefferson scored only four points when N.C. State whipped Duke 87-75 last Sunday at PNC Arena.

On Tuesday night, Jefferson played well offensively, with 14 points and 12 rebounds, but Duke lost 90-74 as Miami ended the Blue Devils' 41-game winning streak at Cameron Indoor Stadium.

Jefferson was a key voice in players-only meetings the Blue Devils held between the Miami loss and Saturday's game at Louisville. But perhaps just as important was his decision to become a larger factor on offense.

"For me it was about finding open spots and when I get the ball, being aggressive," Jefferson said. "Sometimes I don't look to the basket, but today it was about being aggressive and attacking."

Louisville plays a matchup zone defense, which Jefferson called "unique." But he and 6-11 freshman center Jahlil Okafor were able to find space to get to the basket.

Okafor scored 18 points, making 8 of 10 shots, and also received credit from Jefferson.

"Jah, when they were doubling him, did a great job of finding me," Jefferson said. "He pretty much gave me layups because the passes were so good. I was just trying to finish."

Jefferson didn't always get a chance to finish those plays with made baskets as Okafor finished with just one assist. But Jefferson drew fouls on those

Amile Jefferson denies Notre Dame's Steve Vasturia of an easy bucket during Duke's 90-60 rout of the Fighting Irish February 7. Jefferson recorded a career-high 26 blocks during the season. (Jon Gardiner/ Duke Photography)

plays and made seven of his nine free throws.

When he did get shots off, he was close to perfect with six makes on seven tries.

In addition, Duke played a zone defense that clogged the lane and made things difficult on Montrezl Harrell, Louisville's All-American forward from Tarboro, North Carolina. Harrell made 4 of 10 shots for 10 points.

Jefferson is becoming an important factor in the middle as opposing teams spend so much time and effort trying to slow Okafor, Duke's preseason All-American. Jefferson has improved his scoring average to 8.9 points per game and has made 67 percent of his shots this season.

His role as a team captain is proving to be just as important. He and Cook, his fellow co-captain, are supposed to lead the team on the court and off. The meetings following the Miami loss were an example of how the Blue Devils needed to get things right mentally to play better physically.

The result was a win that restores the team's luster following uncharacteristic losses to unranked teams.

"A win here isn't just a win," Cook said. "We haven't been playing great basketball since we got back from break, even though we had a couple of wins. Today was a great, defining win for us. A response to a two-game losing streak." ∎

JANUARY 25, 2015 • NEW YORK, NEW YORK
DUKE 77, ST. JOHN'S 68

COACH 1K

Duke Shows Grit in 1,000th Win for Krzyzewski
By Steve Wiseman

Of the many superlatives Duke achieved while winning 16 of its first 18 games this season to land among the nation's top-five teams, a gritty second-half comeback was absent.

Sunday became a day when the Blue Devils delivered that which will also make it a day to go down in basketball history. Trailing by 10 points with a little more than eight minutes to play, the Blue Devils reversed the game's trend with defense and strong moves to the basket to rally past St. John's 77-68 and give coach Mike Krzyzewski his 1,000th career win.

It was just two weeks earlier that Duke saw a second-half deficit against N.C. State balloon to as many as 19 points before the Wolfpack finished off an 87-75 win.

Two nights later, Miami dominated Duke in the second half to beat the Blue Devils 90-74 at Cameron Indoor Stadium.

Just when it looked like the Blue Devils (17-2) were on the way to letting yet another team walk over them late in a game, they found the toughness to not let that happen.

"We just stayed together, I think," Duke senior guard Quinn Cook said. "In the two games that we lost, when we got down double-digits or nine or whatever, I think that we got tight. Coach just stayed positive. Stayed with us.

"We stayed poised. We got stops. We made hustle plays. We got steals. We got rebounds. It was a 40-minute dogfight out there. We wanted to get this one for coach."

Krzyzewski saw his Blue Devils jump to a 21-10 lead on Sunday and take on the look of a team that would gain an easy nonconference win. But St. John's authored the game's first reversal, shooting 54.8 percent in the first half to lead 43-39.

The halftime locker room speech from Krzyzewski was not for the faint of heart, his players said. Yet the message failed to take hold.

St. John's took advantage of some defensive lapses by Duke and a stretch of three consecutive Blue Devil turnovers on offense to build a 53-43 lead with 15:13 to play.

Duke team members hold up signs commemorating Mike Krzyzewski becoming the first head coach in men's Division I basketball to reach the 1,000-win mark with Duke's 77-68 victory over St. John's in New York. (Megan Morr/Duke Photography)

When Sir'Dominic Pointer scored on spinning move in the lane with 8:32 to play, St. John's had a 61-51 lead and Duke looked dead.

That's when things turned on a dime.

"As weak a looks as we had for 20 minutes, how it changed for 8-or-10 minutes," Krzyzewski said. "The looks on our team, they were unbelievable winning looks and that's what the opponent saw, just like they saw weak for 20 minutes. I've not been in a game like that."

With junior forward Amile Jefferson and junior guard Rasheed Sulaimon both saddled with four fouls, Krzyzewski had already put a defensive system in place to try to stem the Red Storm onslaught.

Marshall Plumlee, a 7-foot redshirt junior center, replaced Jefferson to play with 6-11 freshman Jahlil Okafor in a twin tower approach.

Starting guards Cook and freshman Tyus Jones were joined in the backcourt by sophomore Matt Jones, known as a strong defender with some rebounding skills.

Starting at the 8:11 mark, that group gelled to turn the game in Duke's favor.

It started when Cook drove the lane, sank layup while drawing a foul, and added a free throw.

After Duke limited St. John's to one missed shot, Tyus Jones did the same as Cook. His old-fashioned 3-point play left the Red Storm with a 61-57 lead.

"The first half I just think we weren't as tough as we needed to be," Plumlee said. "Halfway into the second half we started to make those tough plays and come together as a team. Loose balls, defensive stops. That's what made the difference for us."

A sequence just after the game clock ticked below the 7:00 mark proved to be crucial to Duke's win.

Okafor missed a free throw, but Matt Jones grabbed the rebound. He missed a shot only to

NOTABLE: Tyus Jones led Duke in scoring after netting 22 points, with 10 of his points coming at the free throw line. Jones made all 10 of his free throw attempts, making him just the fourth freshman in Duke history to convert double-digit free throw attempts in a game without a miss.

see Cook grab that rebound. Tyus Jones missed a 3-pointer, but Okafor rebounded and scored inside while drawing a foul.

His free throw at the 6:35 mark cut the St. John's lead to 61-60.

Chris Obekpa made one of two free throws giving the Red Storm a 62-60 lead before Cook drilled a 3-pointer with 5:41 left to put Duke in front for good at 63-62.

"People are saying we are young, but we actually learned from our mistakes this time," Matt Jones said. "You saw that the last 10 minutes. We could have quit, but with the leadership from Quinn and Amile and Coach K always having our backs, it was a lot easier. We just made big plays down the stretch."

Duke's march to victory continued with an Okafor basket and a free throw. Tyus Jones sank three free throws after being fouled while attempting a 3-pointer to give Duke a 69-63 lead with 2:54 left.

Tyus Jones' 3-pointer with 1:16 left pushed Duke's lead to 72-65 and sealed St. John's fate as Krzyzewski's victim for win No. 1,000.

Tyus Jones led Duke with 22 points, scoring 11 points over the game's final 7:12. Cook and Okafor scored 17 each.

"We have so many talented players, and each game someone is stepping up," Tyus Jones said. "It's always fun to see. It shows we're always together." ◼

Head coach Mike Krzyzewski addresses the team in the locker room following its 77-68 victory against St John's, which earned Krzyzewski his 1,000th career coaching win. (Megan Morr/Duke Photography)

JANUARY 28, 2015 • SOUTH BEND, INDIANA
NOTRE DAME 77, DUKE 73

ND'S VETS THWART BLUE DEVILS

Irish Seniors Overcome Duke's Precocious Freshmen

By Steve Wiseman

Duke's freshmen were stellar for most of the second half, but Wednesday's battle of top-10 teams belonged to Notre Dame's seniors down the stretch.

Jerian Grant scored 23 points and had 12 assists while Pat Connaughton had 13 points and 12 rebounds as the No. 8 Irish rallied past No. 4 Duke 77-73 in ACC basketball at Purcell Pavilion.

Duke (17-3, 4-3 in ACC) rode hot scoring from its freshmen starters Jahlil Okafor, Tyus Jones and Justise Winslow, to build a 65-55 lead with 10:57 to play.

But the Blue Devils endured a five-minute scoring drought and the Irish ripped off 12 points in a row to regain the lead.

Duke made just 10 of 20 free throws in the game as well, further complicating its chances of knocking off the Irish in their home arena.

"I've just been a poor free throw shooter," said Okafor, who made just 2 of 7 from the line.

Okafor scored 22 points and grabbed 17 rebounds to lead Duke. Tyus Jones had 14 points and

Winslow 13 for Duke. All but three of Duke's second-half points were scored by those three players.

In the final minutes, with the game in doubt, Grant willed Notre Dame (20-2, 8-1 in ACC) to the win.

"He loves the moment," Notre Dame coach Mike Brey said. "He is such a bright lights, big stage guy. He's really clutch."

Grant scored over Okafor after a drive to the hoop to tie the game at 69 with 4:06 left.

Notre Dame's Steve Vasturia hit two free throws with 2:15 left giving Notre Dame a 71-70 lead and Okafor's contested bank shot in the lane bounced off with 1:45 left.

Grant extended the Irish lead to 73-70 as he recovered a loose ball and sank a jump shot as the shot clock expired.

Tyus Jones had tipped the ball away as Grant began a drive to the basket. But the savvy senior recovered and sank a shot that helped subdue Duke.

"That's a heck of a bucket," Duke coach Mike Krzyzewski said. "A fortunate bucket but a heck of a bucket."

Duke senior Quinn Cook's two free throws at 58.4 seconds – the first non-freshmen points of the second half for Duke – sliced Notre Dame's lead to 73-72.

But Grant dribbled the shot clock down, drove the lane to attract the defense and fired a pass to Vasturia in the corner. The sophomore drilled a 3-pointer with 22.9 left giving Notre Dame a 76-72 lead.

"We should not have left Vasturia," Krzyzewski said. "There's two seconds (on the shot clock) and you have to make Grant take a two-point shot, which we were and we left (Vasturia) and the kid made a huge shot."

It was Vasturia's only field goal of the game for a Notre Dame team that made 51.8 percent of its field goals.

Duke's freshmen came roaring out of halftime offensively, spurring a Duke run that gave the Blue Devils a 63-53 lead.

Duke made 9 of its first 14 shots of the second half, with freshmen starters Okafor, Jones and Winslow accounting for all the Blue Devils points over the first eight minutes.

After scoring two points in the first half, Tyus Jones scored 12 points in those eight minutes. His 3-pointer with 12:38 left put Duke up by 10 points.

Winslow scored eight points and Okafor four as Duke's 24-point outburst over eight minutes gave it some breathing room.

"I thought we played winning basketball," Krzyzewski said. "I'm not down on my team about that. But we have to keep learning. We're a young group."

Connaughton kept Notre Dame close, scoring eight points over the first five minutes of the half. His basket tied the score at 49 before Duke scored 14 of the next 18 points behind its fabulous freshmen.

Notre Dame, though, had another offensive punch to throw at Duke. And the Blue Devils helped as they went cold on offense.

A Zach Auguste free throw, followed by a Grant basket after the Irish rebounded Auguste's missed free throw, started a 12-0 Irish run. Demetrius Jackson drilled a 3-pointer from the corner with 9:31 left cutting Duke's lead to 65-61.

Three more empty Duke possessions, including missed 3-pointers by Cook and Matt Jones and a Winslow turnover on a bad pass, kept Notre Dame with the momentum.

Jackson's layup at 8:03 left Duke up 65-63.

Following a missed jumper by Duke's Rasheed Sulaimon, Auguste scored over Okafor in the lane to tie the game at 65-all with 7:01 to play.

With 6:24 left, Grant scored in the lane to put Notre Dame up 67-65.

"Everything coach preaches to us about the little things," Cook said, "they came up and bit us."

Okafor ended Duke's five-minute scoring drought at 5:31 with a basket in the lane.

His basket in traffic with 4:31 left put Duke back in front at 69-67.

Duke's next three possessions saw Okafor go to the free throw line. He made just 1 of 5, missing the front end of a one-and-bonus along the way. His two misses with 2:42 left came with Duke holding a 70-69 lead.

Notre Dame regained the lead 27 seconds later and Duke never caught back up. ■

DUKE'S ROUGH WEEK CONTINUES AS NO. 2 VIRGINIA AWAITS

By Steve Wiseman • January 30, 2015

From the celebration of Mike Krzyzewski's 1,000th win on Sunday to the despair of a tough road loss at No. 8 Notre Dame on Wednesday to the shock of Rasheed Sulaimon's dismissal on Thursday, it's been quite a week for Duke.

Now that the weekend is here, all the Blue Devils have to do is face perhaps their toughest road trip of the season.

No.4 Duke's challenging week continues with a game at No. 2 Virginia Saturday in Charlottesville, Virginia.

The Blue Devils (17-3, 4-3 in ACC) will have to straighten things out mentally in a hurry. The 77-73 loss at Notre Dame came after Duke held a 10-point second-half lead before fading down the stretch.

Less than 24 hours later, Sulaimon was kicked off the team for what Krzyzewski, in a prepared statement, called an inability to "consistently live up to the standards required to be a member of our program."

By Friday, the Blue Devils — with a shortened roster — were en route to Virginia for a battle of top-five teams that's one of the ACC's biggest regular-season games of the season.

Following the loss at Notre Dame, Krzyzewski wasn't highly critical of his team.

"I thought we played winning basketball," Krzyzewski said. "But we have to cash in on the opportunities that are free and the opportunities that are close. Hopefully we'll get that."

Duke made just 10 of 20 free throws, with freshman center Jahlil Okafor hitting only 2 of 7. Forward Amile Jefferson was 0 for 3.

Also, Okafor made 10 of 18 shots, missing several shots in the lane and around the basket.

Still, Duke scored 24 points over the first eight minutes of the second half to build a 63-53 lead.

"We played well," Jones said. "We played well enough to win the game and should have won the game. It hurts because at Miami and N.C. State (which beat Duke earlier this month) we didn't play well. (At Notre Dame) we played well and had the lead for most of the game."

After Jones sank a 3-pointer to put Duke up 63-53 with 12:45 to play, the Blue Devils scored just 10 points the rest of the game.

Krzyzewski pointed to a couple of key sequences where the Blue Devils could have secured the win.

Up 10 points, the Blue Devils ran an in-bounds play under their basket with seven seconds left on the shot clock. But Matt Jones turned the ball over in the lane.

"We lost the ball and were in position to get fouled or to get a three-point play," Krzyzewski said.

The Duke coaching staff, comprised of assistant coach Jon Scheyer (left), head coach Mike Krzyzewski (middle left), associate head coach Jeff Capel (middle right) and assistant coach Nate James (right), looked to refocus the team following its 77-73 loss to Notre Dame and with a tough road game with Virginia on the horizon. (Raashid Yassin/Duke Blue Planet)

"That was a huge play right there."

A few minutes later, Notre Dame's Zach Auguste made one free throw and missed the second. But Irish senior Pat Connaughton grabbed the rebound, which led to a Jerian Grant layup.

"Those two exchanges, if you do them right, you're up 12 or 13, or at the very least you're up 10 with the ball," Krzyzewski said. "That's what happens in games. You have to beat other people when they are playing well. They are good and they are playing well."

Duke will try to play well with just three reserve players available for the rest of the season.

Duke's usual starting lineup consists of freshmen Okafor, Tyus Jones and Justise Winslow, with team captains Quinn Cook and Jefferson. The three remaining players on the bench are Matt Jones, redshirt junior center Marshall Plumlee and freshman Grayson Allen.

Duke also has walk-ons Sean Kelly and Nick Pagliuca on the bench with Sean Obi, who is sitting out this season as a transfer, in street clothes for home games. NCAA rules prohibit players sitting out as transfers from traveling with the team to road games.

Sulaimon had been playing 19.6 minutes per game. In ACC play, he averaged 9.8 points per game while hitting 12 of 24 (50 percent) 3-pointers.

Allen hasn't seen more than eight minutes of play in any ACC game this season. But the move with Sulaimon means that's about to change, starting with the showdown in Charlottesville. ■

JANUARY 31, 2015 • CHARLOTTESVILLE, VIRGINIA
DUKE 69, VIRGINIA 63

UNBEATEN NO MORE

Down 9, Duke Rallies with 3s, Beats No. 2 Cavs

By Steve Wiseman

Every reason existed for No. 4 Duke to lose Saturday night.

On the road at the nation's No. 2 team that's known for stingy defense, the Blue Devils' shots weren't falling and they fell into a double-digit hole.

The Blue Devils were playing with only eight available players, their new reality after junior Rasheed Sulaimon was kicked off the team for disciplinary reasons 48 hours earlier.

Duke's confidence, though, never wavered in these dire circumstances.

"We have winners on this team," Duke sophomore Matt Jones said. "We never give in. Tonight we proved what we are capable of."

It took until the final five minutes but, yes, Duke proved its resiliency.

After missing their first nine 3-pointers of the game, the Blue Devils made five over the game's final five minutes, scoring the game's final 11 points to stun previously unbeaten Virginia 69-63 at John Paul Jones Arena.

"For our guys to have the toughness and the wherewithal to win tonight says a lot about our team," said Duke coach Mike Krzyzewski, whose team scored on 14 of its final 15 possessions.

Things looked bleak for Duke (18-3, 5-3 in ACC) as Virginia's home crowd roared with full throat when the Cavaliers (19-1, 7-1 in ACC) erased the Blue Devils' 26-25 halftime lead to build a 41-30 lead early in the second half.

Virginia's lead was still 11 points before Tyus Jones finally sank Duke's first 3-pointer with 9:37 to play in the game.

Mixing two different zone defenses after Virginia's offense carved up their man-to-man sets earlier in the half, the Blue Devils combined defensive stops with some conversions of their own to trail 49-47 with 6:24 to play.

Virginia responded as London Perrantes sank a 3-pointer and Duke's Justise Winslow was called for a flagrant-1 foul after he missed a shot and grabbed Justin Anderson's leg to prevent him from running back up court.

Justise Winslow rises up for a jumper over a Cavalier defender in the second half of Duke's game against Virginia. Winslow recorded his first double-double of the season after netting 15 points and collecting 11 rebounds en route to a crucial road win for Duke over a top-five opponent. (Raashid Yassin/Duke Blue Planet)

Anderson hit two free throws and Anthony Gill scored inside to put Virginia up by nine, 56-47, with 5:18 left.

All was not lost for the Blue Devils, though.

"We kept believing in each other and we didn't give up," Duke senior Quinn Cook said. "We strung some stops together and were fortunate enough to get some shots to go in. Coach kept believing in us and kept confidence in us. As a player, that does a lot for you. Guys were talking to each other and we stayed together."

Freshman guard Tyus Jones started the comeback with a traditional 3-point play as he drove the lane, hit a bucket, drew a foul and sank a free throw.

Cook's 3-pointer, one of three he would sink the final 4:36, left Virginia's crowd nervous. Jahlil Okafor tipped in Tyus Jones' missed 3-pointer with 4:00 left and Duke was in the game, trailing 58-55.

When Malcolm Brogdon hit a 3-pointer for Virginia, Cook answered with one of his own 17 seconds later.

Virginia's Justin Anderson slammed home two points on a lob pass from Perrantes over the Duke zone and the Cavaliers led 63-58 with 2:59 left.

But Virginia wouldn't score again as Duke saved its lethal scoring punch for crunch time.

Matt Jones sank his only 3-pointer of the game and Winslow stole the ball from Perrantes as he tried to score in the lane.

At the other end, Tyus Jones found a way to zip a pass through Virginia's defense to Winslow under the basket. Winslow's hoop tied the game at 63-all with 2:10 to play.

The Blue Devils bothered Virginia's Anthony Gill into a missed layup with 1:34 left and took possession looking for the lead.

They worked the ball inside to Okafor, who endured hounding double-teams all night. Okafor tossed the ball back out to the perimeter to Cook, who nailed a 3-pointer with 1:15 to play to put Duke in front for good at 66-63.

"There were a few possessions where I thought we were a little stagnant and didn't get the looks we wanted against their zone," Cavaliers coach Tony Bennett said. "I thought there was enough offense there to win that game. At the end you've got to come up with some tough stops. Those errors and breakdowns cost us."

After Virginia's Mike Tobey missed a free throw, secured the rebound and eventually missed a shot in the paint, Duke worked the clock down until Tyus Jones sank a 3-pointer with 9.9 seconds to play to give Duke a 69-63 lead.

That's when the Blue Devils, particularly longtime friends Tyus Jones and Okafor, let loose with celebrations by flexing and gyrating near half-court.

A week that began in New York on Sunday with Krzyzewski's 1,000th career win, then continued with a tough road loss at Notre Dame on Wednesday and Sulaimon's stunning dismissal on Thursday ended with yet another big-time Duke win.

The Blue Devils now own three road wins this season over teams ranked in the Associated Press top 10 – Wisconsin, Louisville and Virginia.

All this from a team that has four freshmen among its eight available scholarship players.

"I really love my team," Krzyzewski said. "They are really tough kids. They are young and we're not that big. We're good. We're not great.

"We have the potential to be very good. But we're not there yet. As long as they keep working at it. But I like my group a lot." ∎

Quinn Cook attempts a 3-pointer over Virginia's Isaiah Wilkins. Cook connected on three of his four attempts from beyond the arc, with all three coming in the final five minutes of the game. Cook's last made three, with 1:19 on the clock, broke the tie and gave Duke the lead. (Raashid Yassin/Duke Blue Planet)

NOTABLE: The victory over second-ranked Virginia was Duke's third road win against a top-10 opponent, the first time in program history a Duke team achieved such a feat.

FEBRUARY 7, 2015 • DURHAM, NORTH CAROLINA
DUKE 90, NOTRE DAME 60

ALMOST PERFECT

Duke Rocks Notre Dame, Shoots 81 Percent in First Half

By Steve Wiseman

Jahlil Okafor's most influential dunk didn't register on the Cameron Indoor Stadium scoreboard Saturday.

Duke's most impressive stretch of basketball came with its 6-11 All-American center watching from the bench.

Despite those oddities being true, the No. 4 Blue Devils did something in their 90-60 rout of No. 10 Notre Dame that left their Hall of Fame coach of 35 years marveling.

"The first half," Mike Krzyzewski said, "was something to behold."

Okafor picked up two fouls and hit the bench just eight minutes into the game. One of the fouls came on an aggressive move through the lane that resulted in a thunderous dunk, which was wiped out by an offensive foul call.

Just 16 seconds later, Okafor picked up foul No. 2 playing defense.

Duke led 17-9 at that point. By the time halftime arrived without Okafor seeing another minute of play, Duke's lead was 50-24.

"We haven't executed that way in a long time," Krzyzewski said. "It was almost...perfect."

Shooting. Defending. Passing.

The Blue Devils (20-3, 7-3 in ACC) did it all with aplomb on Saturday, particularly in the first half Duke made 14 of its first 18 shots, including 7 of 8 3-pointers to lead 43-13. The Blue Devils finished the first half having made 17 of 21 shots for an astonishing 81 percent shooting display. They handed out 11 assists on those 17 made field goals.

They limited Notre Dame (21-4, 9-3) to 36.4 shooting and their lowest point total in the first half of any game this season.

"They really contested and pressured the ball," Notre Dame coach Mike Brey said. "They were so good on the ball screen and that's so important to us. I thought Okafor was better on the ball screen than I had seen him all season."

That's, of course, when Okafor was in the game.

And that brings us back to his dunk that didn't count on the scoreboard.

Such an aggressive and powerful move, even when a foul disqualified it, resonated with his teammates.

Jahlil Okafor scores two of his 20 points in a lopsided home win over No. 10 Notre Dame. Okafor reached the 20-point mark despite playing just 23 minutes in the game due to foul trouble. [Jon Gardiner/Duke Photography]

"I told Jahlil at halftime that that dunk really set the tone," Duke freshman forward Justise Winslow said. "Even though they called an offensive foul. From there, we kind of just took it and ran with it. He picked up his second foul (16 seconds later). But I felt like after that play we just took off."

That Duke did.

An eight-point lead with Okafor on the bench appeared tenuous against a Notre Dame team that averages 80.8 points per game.

Instead, the Blue Devils scored 26 of the game's next 30 points to establish a 30-point lead.

Quinn Cook hit a 3-pointer and Tyus Jones zipped a nifty pass to Marshall Plumlee, Okafor's replacement, for a dunk.

Matt Jones, on his way to scoring 15 of his career-best 17 points in the first half, sank a 3-pointer before driving the lane to draw a foul and make two free throws.

That 10-point outburst, covering just 2:16, gave Duke a 29-11 lead and foreshadowed what the rest of the half would look like for the doomed Irish.

Matt Jones and Cook hit back-to-back 3-pointers just 18 seconds apart to push Duke's lead to 35-13. That started a 16-0 run that Duke needed just 3:17 to complete.

Okafor, watching from the bench, could only cheer along with the rest of the Cameron crowd.

"It was a lot of fun," Okafor said. "I felt like I was on the floor with the guys. Even though I wasn't, it was great seeing my teammates out there having a blast."

Said Krzyzewski, "I liked the fact that our guys, when we got some lead, didn't let up. Notre Dame isn't going to lie down. They're going to come back at us."

The Irish did chip away, cutting Duke's lead to 60-42 early in the second half.

But the Blue Devils unleashed another scoring burst, ripping off 12 consecutive points over the next two minutes and 12 seconds to build their lead back to 30 points at 72-42.

"We had one little segment in the second half that looked like us," Brey said, "but they quickly answered."

Despite sitting out the final 11:57 of the first half after picking up two fouls, Okafor scored 20 points with 10 rebounds. He played just 23 minutes of the game.

Winslow also recorded a double-double by scoring 19 points with 11 rebounds.

Duke's third freshman starter, guard Tyus Jones, scored 12 points and collected seven assists.

Having lost to the Irish 11 days earlier, a 77-73 decision at South Bend, Indiana, Duke resoundingly reversed things with good communication on defense in addition to its lights-out shooting.

"We did a better job of talking and helping and making those guys work," Duke senior guard Quinn Cook said. "We got it going and we didn't let up on the talking. A lot of times when we get a lead we don't talk as much. We play the score. But we didn't do that at all tonight and it paid off."

Duke finished with a 60.8 shooting percentage, including 9 of 15 on 3-pointers.

"I've seen them play a bunch," Brey said, "and this has to be one of their best outings. They got into our lane way too easily."

Notre Dame, which entered the game averaging 80.8 points per outing while shooting 52.1 percent for the season, shot 39.7 percent — its second-worst shooting day of the season.

"I thought we played great man-to-man (defense)," Krzyzewski said. "We will play better defense when we are talking and communicating and playing hard. The word we try to use is 'together.' Just be together." ∎

Matt Jones celebrates on the defensive end of the floor during the first half of Duke's win over Notre Dame. Jones posted a career day, scoring 15 of his career-high 17 points in the opening half. (Jon Gardiner/Duke Photography)

12 FORWARD

JUSTISE WINSLOW

Freshman Puts Pain Aside to Contribute to Duke's Surge
By Steve Wiseman • February 8, 2015

Jahlil Okafor is one of the favorites to be named national player of the year. He and point guard Tyus Jones are included in the midseason watch list for the John Wooden Award.

Duke's third freshman starter, Justise Winslow, is contributing lately at a level where perhaps he should be in those conversations.

Over his last three games, the 6-7 Winslow has recorded three consecutive double-doubles, averaging 16.1 points and 11 rebounds per game.

That includes Saturday's 90-60 win over Notre Dame, when Winslow helped the No.4 Blue Devils with 19 points and 11 rebounds.

Heading into Duke's game at Florida State, it's apparent that Winslow is giving the Blue Devils (20-3, 7-3 in ACC) yet another offensive weapon for opponents to worry about.

His production lately came after he suffered through a tough stretch and after his Duke teammates and coaches asked him to be more aggressive with drives into the lane on offense.

"With my body and my physicality, I can pretty much get into the lane at will," Winslow said. "When I have that mindset, it's easier because I'm not thinking about my shot or my jump shot or anything. I'm just thinking about getting into the lane and making plays."

Winslow appeared ready for ACC play when he scored 13 points and grabbed seven rebounds in Duke's 85-62 win over Boston College in the league opener on Jan. 3.

Justise Winslow releases a floater in traffic during Duke's convincing 90-60 win over Notre Dame in Cameron Indoor Stadium. Winslow would finish with his third-straight double-double after scoring 19 points and bringing down 11 rebounds. (Jon Gardiner/Duke Photography)

Four nights later, at Wake Forest, Winslow scored a season-best 20 points while grabbing seven rebounds as Duke beat the Demon Deacons 73-65.

But Winslow slumped over Duke's next five games, a stretch that included losses at N.C. State and at home against Miami. In those five games, Winslow made just 7 of 30 shots, including 3 of 15 3-pointers, while averaging 4.4 points and 3.2 rebounds.

Part of the reason for his decline in production falls on shoulder and rib ailments. Winslow bruised his shoulder and ribs while diving to the court or being knocked down during games. The bruised ribs affected him more and he still wears padding under his jersey to protect them from further injury.

He said last week that he doesn't expect the injuries to slow his play the rest of the season.

After the Notre Dame win on Saturday, he explained his mindset in dealing with the injury is mind over matter.

"The pain is the pain," Winslow said. "But when you are focusing, you are pretty much locked into the game. Those things fade away. Coming into every game and every practice, I just try to stay emotionally engaged and try not to think about it."

With Okafor (18.2 points, 9.2 rebounds) among the nation's most productive interior players and Jones (11.1 points, 5.1 assists) contributing mightily on the perimeter, Winslow is showing he has a place as well in Duke's drive for ACC and NCAA championships.

"Justise has just played so well," Duke coach Mike Krzyzewski said. "He has really learned to play through his injuries. That's a sign of a guy (who is) really growing up and becoming an outstanding player. You've got to play a little sore without talking about it, and that is what he is doing." ∎

Justise Winslow drives to the basket during Duke's first meeting with the Badgers. Winslow scored 492 points on the year, tied for the eighth-most by a Duke freshman. (Mike Bradley/Duke Blue Planet)

FEBRUARY 18, 2015 • DURHAM, NORTH CAROLINA
DUKE 92, NORTH CAROLINA 90 (OT)

CLASSIC RIVALRY GAME

Duke Scores Last 9 Points of Regulation to Defeat Heels

By Steve Wiseman

Both Duke and North Carolina built double-digit leads only to see the other erase them.

Duke's rally came late, as freshman Tyus Jones scored the No. 4 Blue Devil's final nine points of regulation to send the fierce rivals to overtime.

The lead changed six times in the extra five minutes before the No. 15 Tar Heels ran out of answers.

Behind 22 points each from senior Quinn Cook and Jones, his backcourt mate, the Blue Devils won a classic battle in their storied rivalry, 92-90 in overtime Wednesday night at Cameron Indoor Stadium.

"I love my team," Duke coach Mike Krzyzewski said after the Blue Devils (23-3, 10-3 in ACC) won their sixth game in a row and their ninth in their last 10. "I love my team. They were real men down the stretch."

They had to be to top UNC (18-8, 8-5), which stood toe-to-toe with the Blue Devils in a tough road environment only to fall short at the end.

"The rivalry spoke for itself," Duke freshman center Jahlil Okafor said. "It was magical."

Fueled by hot shooting early and five first-half 3-pointers by Cook, Duke led by as many as 11 in the first half before taking a 49-42 halftime lead.

A scary ankle injury suffered by Okafor late in the first half complicated things for the Blue Devils. Okafor sprained the ankle and was helped from the court. But he returned and, though hobbled, scored 12 points with 13 rebounds in 41 minutes of play.

UNC countered in the second half, pounding the ball inside to Kennedy Meeks and Brice Johnson. They each finished with 18 points to lead UNC, which scored 62 points in the paint and needed that production to overcome 2 of

Quinn Cook goes up for a 3-point attempt over North Carolina's Nate Britt in the first half of Duke's 92-90 overtime win in Cameron Indoor Stadium. Cook tied with teammate Tyus Jones to score a game-high 22 points. (Jon Gardiner/Duke Photography)

NOTABLE: Quinn Cook knocked down 6-of-9 3-point field goal attempts as the Blue Devils shot 62.5 percent from 3-point range.

10 3-point shooting. Reserve Joel James added six points and five rebounds in his 12 minutes.

"It was a nice battle," Okafor said. "They have a bunch of great bigs. Meeks is a huge guy. So is James. It was a lot of fun."

Okafor could only have that sunny perspective because of fellow freshman Tyus Jones' exploits late in regulation.

UNC led 77-67 with 3:50 to play and had Duke on the edge of losing. But Blue Devils freshman Justise Winslow sank a 3-pointer with 3:02 to play.

Winslow drew Duke closer with a dunk and, after Marcus Paige missed a finger roll for UNC, Tyus Jones hit a tough layup with 1:24 left cutting UNC's led to 79–74. That started a streak of nine consecutive points for Duke by Jones.

"He's got cold blood in his veins," Cook said of Tyus Jones. "It's amazing. It's amazing to watch."

A missed free throw by Nate Britt gave Duke a chance and Jones sank two free throws with 1:16 left to leave UNC up 79-76.

With 47.5 seconds left, Johnson sank two free throws.

But Jones answered again for Duke, driving for a basket with 41 seconds left while drawing a foul on Joel Berry. Jones' free throw cut UNC's lead to 81-79.

With 39.5 seconds left, Johnson missed a free throw and the ball bounced out of bounds off the Tar Heels.

Jones tied the score with 27.8 seconds left with a drive through the lane for a layup

Duke successfully fended off UNC's attempt to win the game in regulation as Paige missed a jumper with three seconds left.

"They made some big plays," UNC coach Roy Williams said. "I thought Tyus and Justise were really huge for them down the stretch."

In the extra period, baskets inside by Isaiah Hicks and J.P. Tokoto put UNC up 87-84.

But Tyus Jones drove for a basket and, after a Paige turnover, Cook scored after a drive to put Duke up 88-87 with 2:15 left.

Hicks' free throws gave UNC a one-point lead, but Okafor's basket inside with 1:41 to play put Duke (23-3, 10-3) back in front 90-89.

Nate Britt missed a driving layup with 1:12 left and Jones missed a jumper for Duke with 40 seconds left. But Matt Jones grabbed the rebound for Duke.

Cook was fouled with 31.8 seconds left and the senior guard sank one free throw to give Duke a 91-89 lead.

The Tar Heels moved the ball around as Duke's defense hounded them before Hicks missed a baseline jumper with six seconds to play. Cook grabbed the rebound and was fouled.

Cook made one free throw with 5.2 seconds left, giving Duke a 92-89 lead.

UNC called timeout with 4.7 seconds left and, after the Heels inbounded the ball, Duke's Matt Jones fouled Britt with 3.5 seconds left.

Britt hit the first free throw and missed the second. Paige got his hands on the rebound to the left of the basket, but Duke grabbed the rebound and time expired.

"It was a great game," Krzyzewski said. "One team had to win and one team had to lose and it's one possession and we won. I thought both teams played their hearts out. I don't know how either team could have played any harder than they did." ∎

Tyus Jones drives to the hoop with under a minute remaining in regulation and Duke trailing by five. Jones converted a 3-point play with 41 seconds remaining and knotted the score at 81 with another driving layup less than 15 seconds later to push the game into overtime. (Jon Gardiner/Duke Photography)

MARCH 7, 2015 • CHAPEL HILL, NORTH CAROLINA
DUKE 84, NORTH CAROLINA 77

SWEEPING THE HEELS

Tyus Jones Bounces Back From Injury to Rally Duke

By Steve Wiseman

Be it due to injury or foul trouble, No. 3 Duke often had to patch together a five-man unit to face rival North Carolina Saturday night.

In the end, the Blue Devils did exactly what they've done for the last six weeks and won again.

After missing part of the second half after taking a hard fall on the court and suffering back spasms, Tyus Jones scored 24 points and hit all 12 of his free throws as Duke beat UNC 84-77 at the Smith Center for its 11th consecutive win.

Jones, Duke's freshman point guard, left the game for nearly three minutes as he was slow to get up after driving to make a contested layup and falling hard. A temporary return of back spasms he suffered as a junior in high school gave him pause.

But he returned for the game's final 10 minutes as Duke (28-3, 15-3 in ACC) finally took control of another back-and-forth game between the two rivals. Jones scored 11 points over those final 10 minutes and drew praise from Duke coach Mike Krzyzewski for playing like some of

the best point guards the program has produced.

"I've seen it from a freshman," Krzyzewski said. "Amaker. Hurley. That's it. That's where he is. Tyus is outstanding. He's a big-time player."

As has been the case during its winning streak, which stretches back to Jan. 31, Duke had plenty of outstanding performances from its eight-man playing rotation.

Senior guard Quinn Cook added 20 points, hitting four 3-pointers, while freshman center Jahlil Okafor had 14 points and fellow freshman Justise Winslow added 13 points before fouling out.

The real turning point of the game, though, came when Jones was out with his back injury, Winslow was on the bench with four fouls and Okafor was also getting a rest.

Jones' shot on which he was injured cut UNC's lead, which was as many as seven points, to 49-48.

With UNC up 51-48, Duke's five-man grouping of Grayson Allen, Amile Jefferson, Matt Jones, Marshall Plumlee and Cook

Justise Winslow beats two Tar Heel defenders for an easy pair of points against North Carolina in Chapel Hill. Duke won the regular-season series against the Tar Heels after defeating them on the road, 84-77. (Jon Gardiner/Duke Photography)

ripped off eight consecutive points to put Duke in front for good.

It started with Jefferson's tip-in of an Allen miss, and Matt Jones hit a 3-pointer to put Duke up 53-51 with 11:53 left.

The Blue Devils would never trail again.

"Sometimes things just happen," Krzyzewski said. "It's not coaching. They make it happen. Like, Matt. He only has one bucket in the game. We're down 51-50 and he steps back and knocks that thing down. I love that."

During an official time out with 11:41 to play, Krzyzewski decided to leave that group in instead of replacing them with the normal starters.

Allen, a freshman guard, added another 3-pointer with 11:20 left to complete the 8-0 run and put Duke ahead 56-51.

"These guys, we're winning because of those guys," Krzyzewski said he told his staff. "Let's keep them in."

That's when Allen hit his 3-pointer.

Tyus Jones' back felt good enough to return a minute later and UNC (21-10, 11-7) was unable to ever catch back up.

UNC cut Duke's lead to a point at 56-55, but the Blue Devils hit their next six shots in a row to pull away for good. Tyus Jones' basket at 5:29 gave Duke a 70-61 lead.

"Something went wrong," UNC freshman Justin Jackson said. "I know there was a big turnover that I had that they ended up having two 3s on the next two possessions to put it up by nine. I think, I don't know what it was, we got lackadaisical, just stopped playing. But against a team like that, you can't do that."

Duke made 10 of 10 free throws over the final

NOTABLE: The Blue Devils shot 21-of-26 (.808) from the free throw line, the fifth regular season game that Duke connected on over 80.0 percent of its free throw attempts. Tyus Jones was a perfect 12-of-12 from the free throw line to set a Duke freshman game record for consecutive free throws made without a miss.

Tyus Jones led Duke in scoring with a season-high 24 points, including 17 in the second half of play as Duke outscored the Tar Heels 53-44 after intermission. He also had six rebounds and seven assists to become the first Duke freshman to record at least 20 points, five rebounds and five assists in his first two games against the Tar Heels. Jones averaged 23.0 points, 6.5 rebounds and 7.5 assists per game, while going 18-of-19 (.947) from the free throw line in two meetings with North Carolina.

2:18 to seal the win and sweep its rival and ride its winning streak into the ACC Tournament.

"I have a special group of guys," Krzyzewski said. "I'm not saying we're great. But we have a special group of guys."

UNC turned the ball over 16 times with Duke recording seven steals. The Blue Devils scored 21 points off of UNC turnovers.

"I'm tired of saying this," UNC coach Roy Williams said, "but congratulate Duke. They did some really good things."

Paige scored 23 points to lead the Tar Heels. Brice Johnson added 17, and Jackson scored 14. ■

With a swift step, Jahlil Okafor gets some space as he attempts a reverse layup on the offensive side of the floor against the Tar Heels. Okafor shot 7-of-9 from the field in the contest. (Jon Gardiner/Duke Photography)

ROAD RAGE: SUCCESS IN HOSTILE ENVIRONS PAVED WAY FOR TITLE RUN

By John Roth

For a literal application of Robert Frost's literary road less traveled, consider Duke's final regular-season venture outside the Triangle area.

With a bout of winter weather bearing down on the region, the Blue Devils eschewed the convenience and efficiency of their normal chartered aircraft and instead utilized the services of a Champion Coach bus for their February trek to Virginia Tech.

The early evening ride to Blacksburg the night before the game was uneventful enough with the cruise up into the Virginia mountains requiring barely three hours. Not so the return trip. With the snowstorm at its peak in the wee hours after midnight, it took the Blue Devils a full five hours to negotiate their way down from the Eastern Continental Divide and come sledding to a stop at the front door of Cameron Indoor Stadium — at which point the steely-nerved bus driver received a well-earned round of applause. Durham travel conditions remained so hazardous, however, that several members of the Duke contingent were unable to head home, holing up at the gym until well after sunrise.

It was hardly a conventional road trip for the Blue Devils, except in one significant aspect: although

Duke played some of its worst defense of the season and was taken into overtime by a team that would finish with a 2-16 ACC record, the Devils were still able to come home with a victory.

Tested in virtually every conceivable way on its many out-of-town excursions during the 2015 season, Duke distinguished itself from much of the national pack with its raging results on the road. The Blue Devils' 28 regular-season victories included 13 earned away from the friendly confines of Cameron Indoor Stadium, seven in ACC play and five against teams ranked in the Top 25 at the time. Three wins on the home floors of Top 10 teams undoubtedly played a direct role in Duke receiving a No. 1 seed for the NCAA Tournament.

While head coach Mike Krzyzewski often urges his players never to take victory for granted at home — where Duke lost just once in 2013-14-15 seasons combined — the fact is that almost every top program is successful in defending its home court on a regular basis. Where Duke made its mark in 2015 was on the road.

"When we go on the road we become road warriors," said freshman Justise Winslow. "We don't want to lose. We want to quiet that crowd. We came

Tyus Jones looks to finish after drawing contact from a North Carolina defender. Jones helped guide Duke to a 9-2 record on the road, averaging 14.1 points and 6.0 assists per game in such contests. (Jon Gardiner/Duke Photography)

up short at N.C. State and at Notre Dame, but we just like that environment of going on the road, that opponent team's crowd, and quieting that crowd."

"The mentality that we have to bring when we go into hostile gyms is just toughness and staying together," added senior captain Quinn Cook. "Basketball is a game of runs and when you are on somebody else's home court, their runs can mean more. That can have an effect on the away team with the crowd getting into it. Our team has just been together all year. We play with a chip on our shoulder when we go on the road, like it's us against the world."

Duke's proclivity for producing on the road began well before ACC play with its usual November-December slate of showcase games. The Devils dispatched Michigan State in Indianapolis, won the Coaches vs. Cancer Classic in Brooklyn and knocked off defending NCAA champ Connecticut at the New Jersey Meadowlands all before the Christmas holidays.

But sandwiched in between those neutral territory headliners was Duke's first true road contest — and the first indicator of how this Blue Devil edition might be wired to handle hostile gyms. They took on No. 2 Wisconsin in Madison, where the Badgers almost never fall, and secured an impressive 80-70 decision against a team featuring eventual national player of the year Frank Kaminsky and still riding high off its 2014 Final Four appearance.

When the ACC season hit, Duke had to scramble in the final five minutes to pull out a win in its first league road test at Wake Forest, then fell decisively at N.C. State a few days later. A rare home loss to Miami followed, leaving Duke with a pedestrian 2-2 conference mark headed to Louisville for its first ACC meeting against a hyped Cardinal team that was ranked sixth in the nation. The Blue Devils surprised most observers by coming out in a 2-3 zone defense,

enjoyed a 17-2 run in the first half and got solidly back on track on a day when the season could have turned in a different direction.

Two weeks later Duke headed to second-ranked and undefeated Virginia for another stress test, trying to bounce back from a close loss at Notre Dame. The Cavaliers led by 11 in the second half and by five with three minutes left before Duke reeled off an 11-0 spurt to close the game and win 69-63, stunning a soldout John Paul Jones Arena.

"A defining moment was that Virginia game," Winslow said. "We were down, trailing the whole game, then everyone just came together and we rallied. Those moments in that game and in the locker room after the game, it's something that has kind of defined our team and the mentality we have."

"We stayed positive," Cook noted of the Virginia comeback, during which Duke scored on 14 of its last 15 possessions against one of the nation's stingiest defenses. "Coach kept believing in us and we kept believing in each other, and we were fortunate enough to hit some shots when we needed them the most, and get some stops as well. I just think it was that positive attitude we kept the whole game."

Duke subsequently enjoyed down-to-the-wire road wins at Florida State and Virginia Tech, bracketed around an 80-72 victory at Syracuse before over 35,000 fans. Although former Blue Devil Michael Gbinije poured in 27 points in trying to spark an Orange crush, Duke started the second half on a 13-2 streak and never looked back.

Duke completed the regular season with an 84-77 victory at North Carolina, as the backcourt of Cook and Tyus Jones combined for 44 points and made a plethora of key plays down the stretch for the Blue Devils' fourth win in their last six trips to Chapel Hill. That gave Duke a 7-2 ACC road record for the year, an 11-game winning streak entering the conference tournament, and

Jahlil Okafor rejects Virginia's Malcolm Brogdon during Duke's 69-63 road win over the Cavaliers. Okafor shot nearly 71.0 percent from the field during Duke's road games in the 2014-15 season. (Raashid Yassin/Duke Blue Planet)

a reaffirmation of the Blue Devils' belief in their ability to handle any adverse situation despite their youth and depth-shy roster.

"You have a tremendous opportunity to grow if you are able to win on the road, because there is nothing like a huge road win. Nothing like it, except a tournament win," Krzyzewski said. "So I think it's brought us closer together. I like the fact that our team has been excited to play on the road. They've never been nervous. They've come together to play some of our best basketball of the season."

"There are a lot of things I know I'll always remember," freshman All-America Jahlil Okafor said. "Going to Virginia after just losing at Notre Dame against an undefeated team, going to Wisconsin when everybody thought we were too young and being able to beat them — there have

been a lot of times when our back's been against the wall and we've been able to respond.

"It all goes to Coach K. He gets us mentally ready before the game and he can read all of his players ... so in late-game situations we trust him with our all, and whatever he says goes for us."

"We never give up. We never quit," echoed Winslow. "There's the belief that as long as there's time on the clock we can still win. Everyone trusts each other and everyone's capable of having enough confidence to knock down the big shot or get that big rebound. It's Coach's belief in us, our belief in each other and the trust we have on the team."

That trust helped enable a well-traveled Duke team to plow through almost every road block on its path to a successful regular season, setting the stage for its road to the Final Four and a national title. ∎

EIGHT IS ENOUGH FOR DUKE

By Steve Wiseman • March 8, 2015

Back on Jan. 29, when Duke's roster shrunk to eight players, the Blue Devils' season stood at a crossroad.

Duke had suffered its third ACC loss in seven league contests the night before at Notre Dame.

A game at unbeaten Virginia was two days away.

Rather than crumble, the Blue Devils have thrived, ripping off 11 consecutive wins.

Truly, eight players is enough for Duke to dominate.

Saturday night's 84-77 win at North Carolina that closed the regular season showed how deep Duke is despite its shortened player rotation.

Its three freshmen starters were on the bench for different reasons. Justise Winslow had four fouls. Tyus Jones had injured his back when he hit the court hard after scoring a layup. Jahlil Okafor was getting a rest from banging with the Tar Heels' impressive front line.

UNC led 51-48 and it was up to three guys who hadn't started the game — forward Amile Jefferson, center Marshall Plumlee and freshman guard Grayson Allen — plus a player who had yet to score in the game — sophomore guard Matt Jones — and one starter in senior guard Quinn Cook.

"We know we only have eight guys, but we have eight tremendously talented guys," said Matt Jones, who started the game but not the second half. "Myself, Grayson and Marshall we just try to be ourselves when we got out there. Obviously we don't want to see any of our guys go down. But we have to step up our games, like we've been doing."

That group scored eight consecutive points to put Duke in front for good on its way to a season sweep of the rival Tar Heels.

It started with Jefferson's tip-in of an Allen miss and Matt Jones hitting a 3-pointer to put Duke up 53-51 with 11:53 left.

The Blue Devils would never trail again.

"Sometimes things just happen," Duke coach Mike Krzyzewski said. "It's not coaching. They make it happen. Like, Matt. He only has one bucket in the game. We're down 51-50, and he steps back and knocks that thing down. I love that."

During an official timeout with 11:41 to play, Krzyzewski decided to leave that group in instead of replacing them with the normal starters.

Allen, a freshman guard, added another 3-pointer with 11:20 left to complete the 8-0 run and put Duke ahead 56-51.

"These guys, we're winning because of those guys," Krzyzewski said he told his staff. "Let's keep them in."

That's when Allen hit his 3-pointer.

Quinn Cook addresses the Cameron Indoor Stadium crowd on Senior Night as his teammates look on following Duke's 94-51 win over Wake Forest. (Jon Gardiner/Duke Photography)

"One of the cool things with this group," Krzyzewski said. "I have a special group of guys. I'm not saying we're a great team, but we have a special group of guys. Those three —Justise, Jah and Tyus — are on the bench and they're cheering like crazy for those guys. We have such a together group. It's on them. They really pull for each other."

A glance at the statistical sheet shows all seven of the players — from Plumlee and his seven minutes to Cook, who played 38 — contributed to the win.

Plumlee had two offensive rebounds. Allen had seven points — his 3-pointer and four free throws without a miss. Jefferson's lone basket was that tip-in as part of the key 8-0 Duke run.

The big numbers came from Tyus Jones (24 points), Cook (20 points), Okafor (14 points) and Winslow (13 points).

But all eight are capable of contributing to beating even the toughest teams, which is who Duke will be facing more often than not now that the postseason is here.

"We know we have each other's back," Matt Jones said. "We know that eight is enough. Coach instills that in our mind every day that we are great players. We can get it done. We are very confident in ourselves." ∎

MARCH 12, 2015 • GREENSBORO, NORTH CAROLINA
DUKE 77, N.C. STATE 53

PUMMELING THE PACK

Duke Routs N.C. State, Takes 49-20 Halftime Lead

By Steve Wiseman

Duke's side of the ACC Tournament bracket set up a revenge week.

The three teams responsible for the No.2 Blue Devils' losses are lined up for them.

The first stop on the tour was an early-round knockout that flattened N.C. State Thursday night.

The Blue Devils scored with overwhelming efficiency against the Wolfpack, building a 29-point first-half lead and rolling to a 77-53 ACC Tournament quarterfinal win at Greensboro Coliseum.

By dispatching seventh-seeded N.C. State, which beat Duke 87-75 in Raleigh back on Jan. 11, the Blue Devils (29-3) advance to the semifinals to meet either Miami or Notre Dame on Friday night.

Like N.C. State, the Hurricanes and Irish each logged January wins over Duke, and Duke freshman Justise Winslow couldn't deny the revenge factor.

"To be honest, it was," Winslow said. "But more importantly we wanted to come out and win this. We know it's win or go home. We wanted to come out here and take care of business regardless of who we are playing."

Currently, the Blue Devils look nothing like the team that lost those games. They collected their 12th consecutive win with their wipeout of N.C. State Thursday.

"What we are doing is maturing as a basketball team," Duke coach Mike Krzyzewski said.

Duke scored on 19 of its first 23 possessions, scoring points at an 82 percent clip, over most of the first half of its blowout win. At that point, three seconds short of 16 minutes into the game, Duke had made 17 of 23 shots while committing just one turnover to take a 42-17 lead.

"We did a great job of coming out in a good tempo and playing at our pace," Winslow said. "We came out and set a tone and never eased up."

Duke served notice early of its intention to advance in the ACC Tournament. The Blue Devils scored the game's first seven points — one of three 7-0 runs they would produce in the first half.

After a Ralston Turner 3-pointer for N.C. State, Duke ripped off six more points in a row and had its first double-digit lead at 13-3 just 4:10 into play.

Turner scored back-to-back baskets, one of the few times the Wolfpack would score on consecutive possessions in the first half, to cut Duke's lead to 15-9.

But Duke needed just a minute and a half to score seven more points in a row on two Winslow free throws, a Quinn Cook 3-pointer and reserve guard Grayson Allen's driving layup for a 22-9 Blue Devils lead.

N.C. State would never draw closer than 11 points the rest of the game.

When Matt Jones sank two free throws with 7:03 left in the half, Duke led 33-13.

Marshall Plumlee throws down one of his six dunks with authority against N.C. State in Duke's quarterfinal matchup in the ACC Tournament. (Jon Gardiner/Duke Photography)

Two more Matt Jones free throws, at 4:03, made it 42-17.

Duke's largest lead of the half came when Allen sank a 3-pointer with 1:32 left before halftime to put the Blue Devils up 49-20.

The performance was reminiscent of Duke's 50-point first half against Notre Dame at Cameron Indoor Stadium back on Feb. 7. That was the Blue Devils' first game against the Irish after losing 77-73 to them in South Bend, Indiana, on Jan. 28.

Duke has not lost since, including the 90-60 win over Notre Dame that its strong first half at Cameron made possible.

One night after N.C. State guards Cat Barber and Trevor Lacey combined to score 55 points in a win over Pittsburgh, Duke limited them to four points.

Barber was scoreless on seven missed shots while Lacey made just 2 of 8 field goals.

Cook, Tyus Jones and Matt Jones manned the starting guard slots with Allen also providing solid minutes.

Cook, the senior captain, led the defensive effort though as he continues to show he's become a much better defender.

"I was tired of coach getting on me in film about not playing defense," Cook said. "It took me three years to finally realize it, but I am playing defense. It's fun. It's fun. I have learned to enjoy playing great defense, and my teammates have helped me. I'm never playing by myself out there." ∎

MARCH 13, 2015 • GREENSBORO, NORTH CAROLINA
NOTRE DAME 74, DUKE 64

MENTAL LETDOWN

Okafor Scores 28, But Lackluster First Half Dooms Devils

By Steve Wiseman

No. 2 Duke's valiant effort in the second half simply wasn't enough to overcome its poor start Friday night.

Lost on offense during an emotionally disengaged first half, the Blue Devils cut No. 11 Notre Dame's 17-point lead to four points late before losing 74-64 in an ACC Tournament semifinal game at Greensboro Coliseum.

Despite getting 28 points from freshman center Jahlil Okafor, the loss ended a 12-game winning streak for Duke (29-4), and the tournament's second seed was sent home.

"I'm proud of how we played the last 16 minutes, but not how we played before that," Duke coach Mike Krzyzewski said.

No. 3 seed Notre Dame (28-5) will play No. 19-ranked North Carolina (25-10) in the ACC Tournament championship game Saturday night.

"I guess it's only fitting that to get it, you have to go through Duke and North Carolina down here on their turf," Notre Dame coach Mike Brey said of winning the ACC championship.

Krzyzewski saw in the early minutes that his team wasn't where it needed to be mentally or physically to beat Notre Dame. He called a timeout less than two minutes into the game.

"We said three or four things for them to do, and they didn't do any of them," Krzyzewski said. "That is so out of character. It wasn't because they had a bad attitude or anything. We just weren't there mentally. We were trying to get something the whole half."

After his team's lackluster first half, which saw Notre Dame build a 41-26 lead at intermission, Krzyzewski benched two starters — Justise Winslow and Matt Jones — for the start of the second half in favor of junior forward Amile Jefferson and freshman guard Grayson Allen.

"Coach did what he thought was best for the team," Winslow said. "That's what I signed up for. I knew that coach is straightforward with everything. When he didn't start me, I didn't let that hinder me at all. I was ready to get into the game."

The Blue Devils played with more intensity early in the half but could only cut the deficit to 11 points. Duke's perimeter shooting problems kept it from drawing closer as the Blue Devils missed their first three 3-pointers of the second half.

Winslow, though, started to impact the game for the Blue Devils.

He blocked a shot attempt by Notre Dame's Pat

Connaughton, grabbed the rebound and picked up an assist on an Okafor basket at the other end.

With 14:17 left, Winslow's aggressive drive to the basket ended with a slam dunk and a foul on Notre Dame's Bonzie Colson. Winslow added the free throw and Duke trailed 49-39.

After a Colson miss, Winslow's pass to Okafor under the basket resulted in a basket that cut Notre Dame's lead to 49-41 with 13:27 to play.

The Irish held firm for the next eight minutes, refusing to let the inspired Blue Devils draw closer.

But three consecutive Duke baskets, two inside from Okafor sandwiched around a Winslow field goal, helped Duke climb back to within five points at 66-61 with 4:01 to play.

After two Jerian Grant free throws for Notre Dame, Cook missed a 3-pointer, but Winslow rebounded and kicked a pass out to Tyus Jones for a 3-pointer that left Notre Dame with a 68-64 lead and 3:12 left.

With 1:48 left, Okafor had a chance to cut into the deficit more, but he missed two free throws.

A jump shot from 16 feet by Connaughton with the shot clock expiring at 1:12 put the Irish up 70-64 and sealed Duke's fate.

"We didn't play the way we had been playing defensively, and that put us in a hole," Cook said. "They made some plays. Connaughton hit a big shot."

Cook, Duke's senior guard who will finish his Duke career without having won an ACC regular-season or tournament championship, had a tough shooting night. He made just 2 of 12 shots overall and was 1 of 8 on 3-pointers.

Notre Dame shot 53 percent in the first half and finished at 50 percent for the game. Colson, a reserve forward, led Notre Dame with 17 points.

NOTABLE: Jahlil Okafor scored 28 points on 13-of-18 (.722) shooting from the field in Duke's ACC Semifinal loss to Notre Dame. Okafor averaged a double-double in Duke's three meetings with the Fighting Irish, scoring 23.3 ppg on 32-of-47 (.681) shooting and adding 11.7 rpg.

Guard Demetrius Jackson finished with 15 points while Grant had 13.

As hot offensively as the Blue Devils were early in Thursday night's 77-53 quarterfinal win over N.C. State, they were just as cold early against the Irish.

Duke scored on just three of its first 14 possessions, turning the ball over five times and making just 2 of 10 shots, as Notre Dame bolted to an 18-5 lead.

Even though Okafor scored 15 points in the first half, Duke got little else in terms of offensive production as the Irish took a 41-26 lead at halftime.

The Blue Devils hit only 11 of 27 shots (40.1 percent) in the first half. The only 3-pointer Duke made was by Cook, who had seven halftime points.

The Blue Devils only attempted four 3-pointers as Notre Dame's defense was designed to crowd them at the 3-point line to force them to attempt 2-point shots.

Duke finally found a groove in the second half, but the double-digit deficit was too much to overcome.

"They're battling," Krzyzewski said, "just like they have all year. You have to play 40 minutes and we didn't do that." ■

15

CENTER

JAHLIL OKAFOR

NCAA Stage Set for Skilled Big Man
By Steve Wiseman • March 20, 2015

Jahlil Okafor is having the time of his life playing basketball for Duke this season.

His goal now is to keep the good times rolling at the most important time of the season.

Duke's 6-11 center became the first freshman in ACC history to be named the league's player of the year.

He's one of four finalists for the Naismith Award, given to the national player of the year.

He's been named a first-team All-American by *The Sporting News* and the U.S. Basketball Writers Association.

But as Duke faces Robert Morris at Charlotte's Time Warner Cable Arena in an NCAA Tournament South Region game, Okafor has reached the most important part of what figures to be his lone season in a Blue Devils uniform.

"My focus right now is on the tournament," Okafor said Thursday. "When I first decided I wanted to go to Duke University or even the thought of college basketball, I always imagined the opportunity of winning a national championship, and the time is now and this is where I want to be, so all my focus is on this right now."

His status as the top prospect for this summer's NBA Draft will have to wait. Duke hopes it is for six games and three more weeks.

Jahlil Okafor lays it in for two of his nine points in the Regional Final of the NCAA Tournament in Houston, Texas. Duke shot just 37.5 percent from the field in the game, but made 16-of-19 free throw attempts to reach the Final Four. (Jon Gardiner/Duke Photography)

Regardless, Okafor said this season has been a pleasure to be a part of, from the moment he arrived on campus last summer.

"My leaders, Quinn Cook, Amile Jefferson, they've been helping me the whole way," Okafor said.

Okafor is the best player on a Duke team that has thrived thanks to its unity.

The team's captains — Cook and Jefferson — played important roles in developing that unity starting last year.

That can sometimes be difficult with a player as talented as Okafor who enters school with the idea already in his head that he'll likely he staying for one year only.

Still, Duke's 29-4 season and the joy the players show around one another are evidence of their talent and their camaraderie.

That's what Cook and Jefferson wanted to achieve.

"It makes me feel great," Jefferson said. "We've had an amazing season and we have a chance to do something special with that group. So I'm extremely happy with how our team is and the type of chemistry and bond that we were able to grow. It started way, way back in our summer sessions with everybody believing in one another. We built a unity and a trust that a lot of teams don't ever get to see."

Duke coach Mike Krzyzewski said Okafor has been able to learn and grow as a player while competing against tough competition.

"He's grown continuously," Krzyzewski said, "And he's got a lot more growth ahead of him. The main thing for Jah is that he's gotten better as the season's gone along."

The only thing that stunted his development was the sprained ankle he suffered in Duke's 92-90 overtime win over North Carolina on Feb. 18. Okafor missed Duke's next game, a 78-56 win over Clemson, but returned on Feb. 25 to score 30 points in Duke's 91-86 overtime win at Virginia Tech.

Still, Okafor wasn't 100 percent, Krzyzewski said.

"That stopped some of his growth because he's had to compensate," Krzyzewski said.

But in practices this week since the end of the ACC Tournament, Krzyzewski has seen improvement in the way Okafor moves on the court.

"First of all," Krzyzewski said, "he started the last couple practices fluid instead of working his way into it, favoring a little bit the ankle and until he got warmed up, and then his lateral movements were, he didn't think about them, he just did them. You could just tell, there's been a marked improvement."

For all the fun Okafor has had while leading the Blue Devils in scoring (17.7 points) and rebounding (9.0), perhaps his best is still yet to come on the sport's biggest stage.

"Although he's played well," Krzyzewski said, "I think if he can be really healthy for tomorrow's game, I think he can do even better." ∎

Jahlil Okafor lets out a boisterous yell as he heads to the line looking to capitalize on an and-one attempt in overtime against North Carolina in Cameron Indoor Stadium. (Jon Gardiner/Duke Photography)

MARCH 20, 2015 • CHARLOTTE, NORTH CAROLINA
DUKE 85, ROBERT MORRIS 56

AUSPICIOUS DEBUT

Young Devils Rout Robert Morris in Their First NCAA Tourney Game
By Steve Wiseman

Top-seeded Duke downplayed any talk about Mercer or Lehigh and made sure there were no reminders of recent upsets on the court Friday night.

The Blue Devils made 11 of their first 14 shots against No. 16 seed Robert Morris and blew out the Colonials 85-56 in an NCAA Tournament South Region game at Time Warner Cable Arena.

No. 4-ranked Duke (30-4), having been bounced from the tournament without winning a game in two of the last three seasons, easily advanced to the Round of 32. The Blue Devils will play No. 8 seed San Diego State, which beat No. 9 seed St. John's 76-64, on Sunday.

The victim of upsets by teams with double-digit seeds in 2012 (Lehigh) and 2014 (Mercer), Duke flexed its muscles to quickly show the Northeast Conference champion Colonials they wouldn't be joining that list.

"I had fun. That's the bottom line," Duke freshman center Jahlil Okafor said. "We came out and played a great game so I enjoyed myself."

Quinn Cook scored 22 points, hitting six 3-pointers, while Okafor scored 21 points for Duke, which shot 63 percent. Tyus Jones, Amile Jefferson and Marshall Plumlee each added 10 points for Duke.

Robert Morris (20-15) had an early 7-5 lead before Duke ran off 11 points in a row to take the lead for good.

Cook, who made his first four 3-pointers of the first half, hit 3-pointers to start and finish that run. Tyus Jones also had a 3-pointer and Matt Jones scored a layup.

After a Robert Morris basket, Tyus Jones hit a jumper and Jefferson and Plumlee scored layups inside to give Duke a 22-9 lead.

At that point, Duke had made nine of its 10 shots.

A basket inside from Okafor and another Tyus Jones basket put Duke ahead 26-9 and the Blue Devils were shooting 79 percent (11 of 14) at that point.

Duke shot 63 percent in the first half, taking a 42-25 lead behind Cook's 14 points.

"Real sharp, real sharp," Tyus Jones said. "Just being ready to play. Right out the gate we

Amile Jefferson slams home a dunk in the waning minutes of Duke's opening game of the NCAA Tournament, one of seven Blue Devil dunks. The Blue Devils outscored Robert Morris in the paint, 46-24. (Jon Gardiner/Duke Photography)

were ready to go. Quinn hit some 3s, Jah got some easy baskets. It was just one of those things where we were locked in and focused and ready to go out the gate."

The game's one bit of drama came in the second half when Duke was up 54-34. Okafor attempted a reverse dunk on fast break and missed. An incensed Duke coach Mike Krzyzewski told Plumlee to enter the game and then called timeout to make sure the sub was made and to yell at his team for showboating.

The Colonials, though, caught fire and ripped off 10 consecutive points to cut its deficit in half.

Rodney Pryor hit two 3-pointers during the run that left Robert Morris down 54-44 with 12:26 to play.

"We went up by 20 points and we got a little lax," Okafor said. "They cut it down to 10. I learned my lesson, also. That's something that Coach always tries to emphasize."

With the score 56-46, Justise Winslow turned the game back into a one-sided rout.

Duke's 6-6 freshman hit a 3-pointer and drove for a layup in transition. He then rebounded another Robert Morris missed shot, drove through the defense and dished a pass in the corner to Tyus Jones, whose 3-pointer put Duke up 64-46.

When Okafor scored inside with 9:33 to play, Duke had matched Robert Morris' 10-0 run and restored its 20-point lead.

Any drama had left the building for good. ■

Marshall Plumlee throws down a resounding dunk as Robert Morris' Lucky Jones looks for cover. (Jon Gardiner/Duke Photography)

NOTABLE: Marshall Plumlee recorded his first career double-double after scoring 10 points (5-of- 6 shooting) and bringing down 10 rebounds.

MARCH 22, 2015 • CHARLOTTE, NORTH CAROLINA
DUKE 68, SAN DIEGO STATE 49

ONE STEP CLOSER

Okafor, Cook and Winslow Lead Blue Devils Past Aztecs

By Steve Wiseman

Duke started Sunday's game in Charlotte like it was eager to get out of town and on to the next assignment.

That spelled doom for San Diego State's upset hopes.

The Blue Devils are the NCAA Tournament South Region's No. 1 seed and they played like it, building a 13-point halftime lead and rolling to a 68-49 win over the No. 8 seed Aztecs at Time Warner Cable Arena.

Duke (31-4) needed less than seven minutes of play to open an 11-point lead and let San Diego State know its task was too tough to handle.

"We know it has to be 40 minutes of great basketball," Duke senior guard Quinn Cook said. "When we start off the game and the second half like we want, we like our chances."

Duke has two freshmen starters who are projected to be lottery picks in this June's NBA Draft. Both had their various talents on display against overwhelmed San Diego State (27-9).

Center Jahlil Okafor scored 26 points, making 12 of 16 shots against an Aztec defense that rated statistically among the nation's best. Forward Justise Winslow added 13 points and 12 rebounds while also contributing five assists, four steals and three blocked shots.

The combination of their talents made Duke impossible to stop.

"It just takes us to a whole other level," Duke coach Mike Krzyzewski said. "Those two kids played at a really high level."

San Diego State coach Steve Fisher last faced Duke in an NCAA Tournament game in 1992 when the Blue Devils routed his Fab Five-led Michigan Wolverines in the national championship game.

He walked away impressed from this latest meeting, too.

"They've got a team full of very good players," Fisher said. "Okafor is a load. He's hard to guard. I think we gave him two, three, four that were too easy, but he's good. He's very, very talented. And again, he's not the Lone Ranger. Winslow can play. They've got a terrific team and they played like a No. 1 seed today."

Quinn Cook attempts to draw contact from San Diego State's Skylar Spencer during Duke's NCAA Third Round game in Charlotte, N.C. (Jon Gardiner/Duke Photography)

Duke will carry that No. 1 seed on to Houston, where the Blue Devils will take part in the South Regional semifinals on Friday night at NRG Stadium. Duke will play No. 5 seed Utah (26-8).

If that game is anything like Duke's two games in Charlotte, the Blue Devils will be in control early.

In Friday's 85-56 win over 16th-seeded Robert Morris, Duke hit 11 of its first 14 shots to blow out the Colonials.

San Diego State felt a similar fate.

"Just play with passion, play together and play hard," Duke forward Amile Jefferson said. "Share emotion and have energy and emotion. If we can do those things, we will be fine. We have the talent. We have the camaraderie, the chemistry and the athleticism to really go out there and lock down. That's what we've displayed in these last two games."

Duke hit 53.4 percent of its shots against San Diego State, giving it a shooting percentage of 58.7 percent for its two NCAA Tournament weekend wins.

While building a 37-24 halftime lead on Sunday, Duke had 10 assists on its 17 made field goals.

Tyus Jones led Duke with six assists in the game while senior guard Quinn Cook had two assists to go with his 15 points.

"Our guards, they were phenomenal tonight on both ends of the floor," Okafor said. "They found me multiple times to give me easy opportunities to score and they were giving me all the confidence in the world, but I think their quickness did give San Diego State a problem."

Once Okafor got the ball, the Aztecs weren't equipped to stop him.

"I played against big players before, but I haven't played against anybody that big, with that skill set," SDSU center Skylar Spencer said.

Defensively, Duke held San Diego State to 32.8 percent shooting overall while recording seven steals.

"We did a great job of putting pressure on the ball handlers," Jefferson said. "They were never able to catch the ball and see space. We were making them catch the ball really far out so they couldn't get into their sets. And our bigs did a great job of protecting the paint." ∎

Okafor records one of his three blocks of the game against San Diego State, denying Winston Shepard. Duke's defense allowed just one Aztec to score double-digit points. [Jon Gardiner/Duke Photography]

NOTABLE: Jahlil Okafor led the Blue Devils with 26 points on 12-of-16 (.750) shooting from the field. Over the first two games of the NCAA Tournament, Okafor shot a combined 21-of-27 (.778) from the floor.

MARCH 27, 2015 • HOUSTON, TEXAS
DUKE 63, UTAH 57

HOMETOWN HERO

Justise Winslow Shines in Front of His Native Houston

By Steve Wiseman

No. 4 Duke had a hometown kid eager to lead and an increasingly tough team defensive mindset on Friday night.

That left underdog Utah without much chance to end the Blue Devils' season.

Houston native Justise Winslow scored 21 points, and top-seeded Duke held Utah to 35 percent shooting as the Blue Devils won 63-57 in an NCAA Tournament South Regional semifinal at NRG Stadium.

Duke (32-4) advances to the tournament's elite eight for the second time in three seasons. The Blue Devils will play No. 2 seed Gonzaga (35-2), which eliminated UCLA 74-62 earlier on Friday night, on Sunday with a spot in the Final Four on the line.

"It's a once in a lifetime experience," Winslow said. "I guess two in a lifetime now, since we won the first game."

Playing in his hometown the day after his 19th birthday, Winslow turned in a stellar game. The 6-6 forward made eight of 13 shots while grabbing 10 rebounds and blocking two shots.

"He played with great emotion," Duke junior forward Amile Jefferson said. "He was everywhere. He was really that piece that we needed. He scored the ball, he made blocks, defensive plays. He was everywhere tonight, and that's the kind of player he is."

Freshman guard Tyus Jones scored 15 points for Duke, which is one win away from its first Final Four appearance since winning the 2010 NCAA championship. Senior guard Quinn Cook added 11 points for Duke, which led by 15 points with eight minutes to play and held off Utah (26-9).

Jones made nine of his 10 free throws, while Cook was seven of eight.

"Our guys came through," Duke coach Mike Krzyzewski said. "I thought our guards showed great poise to hit all those free throws down the stretch — clutch free throws."

Utah's cold shooting (29.6 percent) in the first half allowed Duke to take a five-point halftime lead. The Utes, struggling in the half-court against Duke's defense, hit just 6 of their

Justise Winslow comes down with one of his 10 rebounds during Duke's Sweet 16 game against Utah in his hometown of Houston, Texas. (Jon Gardiner/Duke Photography)

NOTABLE: In his hometown of Houston and one day after his 19th birthday, Justise Winslow scored a team-high 21 points and added 10 rebounds to record back-to-back double-doubles for the third time in the season.

first 18 shots of the second half.

Duke wasn't burning up the nets, but Winslow had the hottest hand and he helped Duke keep a comfortable advantage.

Winslow hit back-to-back 3-pointers, the second coming with 12:24 to play, that gave Duke a 41-32 lead.

Winslow's aggressive drive through the lane for a soaring layup in traffic with 10:36 left gave Duke a 45-34 lead.

After a Winslow steal, Amile Jefferson found an easy lane to the basket as Utah paid too much attention to Jahlil Okafor. Jefferson's emphatic two-handed slam dunk put Duke up 47-34 with 8:51 left.

"Justise made some big-time plays and timely, timely baskets," Krzyzewski said. "That kept us in position where we were in control."

Utah finally broke a five-minute scoring drought with a Jakob Poeltl basket with 7:16 left and a 3-pointer by Brandon Taylor left Duke with a 49-39 lead.

After a Duke turnover, Taylor scored in the lane on Utah's third shot of a possession with 5:27 to play and the Blue Devils' lead was down to 49-41.

Another Duke turnover allowed Utah a chance to draw closer, but Taylor missed a 3-pointer from the right corner.

Blocked shots by Poeltl and Brekott Chapman kept Duke's scoring drought alive, and Poeltl scored inside and the Utes trailed 49-43 with 4:03 to play.

But Winslow, once again, turned in a big play to boost Duke. Winslow muscled inside to score, draw a foul and end a five-minute stretch with no Duke points.

Krzyzewski slapped Winslow a five as the official timeout arrived.

Following the timeout, Winslow sank the free throw and Duke led 52-43 with 3:44 left.

"Coach tells me throughout the season to stay aggressive, try to get to the basket," Winslow said. "If they're sagging off, shoot my bullets. Whenever they

sag off, get to the lane. It's something I'm capable of. At the same time, I'm trying to stay aggressive and just make plays."

Utah's struggles to make shots allowed Duke to lead by as many as 10 points in the first half before taking a 27-22 lead at intermission.

The Utes made just four of their first 21 shots and finished the first half at 29.6 percent (8 of 27). Utah attempted only four 3-pointers, hitting one, over the first 20 minutes.

Utah guard Delon Wright picked up three first-half fouls and was limited to only 13 minutes of play. He scored two first-half points.

Wright, a first-team, All-Pac-12 player, finished the game with 10 points on four of 13 shooting.

"They have a tough backcourt, but we made them work," Cook said. "Taylor got hot at the end. But all in all, we held them in check."

Even though the Utes were struggling to score, Duke's lead was just 19-17 with 5:27 left in the half.

But the Blue Devils went on an 8-0 run to build their first double-digit lead. With Wright on the bench, Krzyzewski had the Blue Devils employ a zone press that caused Utah to turn the ball over on three consecutive possessions.

Cook scored on a driving shot to start the eight-point run. Two Tyus Jones free throws, followed by his bank shot in transition, pushed Duke's lead to 25-17.

Okafor found room in the lane to drive and score with 3:05 to play giving Duke a 27-17 lead.

Utah was in the midst of going four minutes without scoring, and the Blue Devils had chances to build an even larger lead. But the Blue Devils missed three shots and turned the ball over twice and didn't score again the rest of the half.

On the other end, Okafor picked up his first two fouls and Utah reserve center Dallin Bachynski scored a basket and hit three free throws to cut Duke's lead to 27-22 at halftime. ∎

Tyus Jones battles Utah's Brandon Taylor for a loose ball in Duke's Sweet 16 victory. Duke's tenacious defense limited the Utes to 35.0 percent shooting from the field, including 25.0 percent from 3-point range. (Jon Gardiner/Duke Photography)

MARCH 29, 2015 • HOUSTON, TEXAS
DUKE 66, GONZAGA 52

DUKE DELIVERS

Defensive Effort Sends Devils to Their First Final Four Since 2010
By Steve Wiseman

Sunday became a day to treasure for No. 4 Duke.

The Blue Devils treasured the ball against Gonzaga, committing a season-low three turnovers.

They treasured every basket because they were so hard to come by on a day when the Blue Devils shot just 37.5 percent.

In the end, they'll treasure the memories created by clinching yet another Final Four trip in the school's storied basketball history.

Top-seeded Duke led scrappy No. 2 seed Gonzaga most of the way in the NCAA Tournament South Regional final but needed a game-ending kick to secure a 66-52 win at NRG Stadium.

Because the Blue Devils (33-4) won in such a fashion, they are returning to the Final Four for the first time since winning the 2010 NCAA championship. Duke, one of three top seeds in the Final Four along with Kentucky and Wisconsin, will face East Regional champion Michigan State in the national semifinals on Saturday.

"Our coaches, they don't sleep," Duke senior guard Quinn Cook said. "They have us so prepared, it's amazing. To see it everything come together and pay off, it's overwhelming. It's amazing."

Duke rode balanced scoring to the win, with freshman Justise Winslow and sophomore Matt Jones sharing the team lead with 16 points each. Freshman guard Tyus Jones scored 15 points.

Cook, one of the team's captains and the lone scholarship senior, fought through a 2 of 10 shooting day to score 10 points with the help of 5-of-6 free throw shooting.

Matt Jones' points were one off his season high and were a pleasant surprise since he averages just 5.9 points per game this season. His four 3-pointers tied a season high for a single game.

"Matt gave us such a huge lift," Duke coach Mike Krzyzewski said. "He's been that dirty-work guy. For him to hit those four 3s, it's like a big difference."

Matt Jones made one in the first half

Following their 66-52 win over Gonzaga in an Elite Eight contest, head coach Mike Krzyzewski and the Blue Devils were once again cutting down the nets on the way to the Final Four. Duke punched its ticket to the Final Four for the 16th time in program history. (Jon Gardiner/Duke Photography)

when Duke built an 11-point lead and took a 31-26 advantage at intermission.

He sank three more in the second half. The first one was Duke's only made field goal over the first four minutes of the half as Gonzaga's 12-3 run put the Zags in front 38-34.

Matt Jones' second 3-pointer of the half, with 12:53 left in the game, came during a 9-0 run and gave Duke the lead for good at 41-38.

With 9:36 to play, he sank another 3-pointer that gave Duke a 48-42 lead.

"Teams usually lose me in transition or the flow of the offense," Matt Jones said. "Luckily I was able to hit a couple shots and help my team to the victory."

Winslow, playing in his hometown, also scored 16 points. But it was when the bulk of his points came that mattered.

With Duke leading 53-51 with five minutes left, Winslow scored the game's next seven points.

With 4:33 left, he drove the lane to draw a foul and sink two free throws.

After Kevin Pangos missed an open 3-pointer for Gonzaga, Tyus Jones missed a 3-pointer for Duke. But Winslow leaped high to grab the rebound and draw another foul. His two free throws with 3:38 to play put Duke up 57-51.

Kyle Wiltjer missed for Gonzaga and Winslow sank a 3-pointer with 2:45 left giving Duke a 60-51 lead.

The Blue Devils closed the game out by scoring 13 of the final 15 points. Winslow scored the bulk of them.

"For it to be in Houston, me at home in front of my family and friends, it's such a special moment," Winslow said.

Gonzaga played strong enough defense that Duke's 37.5 percent shooting was well below its season average of 50.2 percent.

But the Blue Devils took care of the basketball exceptionally well. They didn't commit their first turnover until 18 minutes into the game, and it came when Jahlil Okafor was called for an offensive foul. The final turnover came in the game's final seconds when, with the outcome decided, the Blue Devils intentionally let the shot clock expire for a violation.

"I think it's incredible," Duke associate head coach Jeff Capel said. "I thought Tyus did a great job of controlling our team and Quinn. It's amazing because I thought Gonzaga played really well defensively."

Duke turned in yet another solid defensive performance of its own. Gonzaga made 44 percent of its shots but was just 2 of 10 on 3-pointers. Duke recorded eight steals as the Zags turned the ball over 13 times.

"I thought Duke played great defense on us," Gonzaga coach Mark Few said. "Stretches in the first half and late stretches in the second half, and that was probably the difference."

And so Duke heads to the 16th Final Four in school history and the 12th of Krzyzewski's 35 years on the job. That ties Krzyzewski with John Wooden for the most Final Fours as a head coach.

The Blue Devils are within two wins of their fifth NCAA championship.

"This is what I have always wanted," said Okafor, the ACC player of the year who scored just nine points on Sunday. "Watching March Madness growing up, you always wanted to be on a team that went to the Final Four and had an opportunity to win a national championship. It's a dream come true for me." ∎

Justise Winslow brings down a rebound with an outstretched arm against Gonzaga in the second half of Duke's Elite Eight win. Winslow's efforts earned him all-tournament team honors. (Jon Gardiner/Duke Photography)

NOTABLE: The win over Gonzaga was Duke's fifth victory over an AP Top 10 opponent and punched the Blue Devils' ticket to the Final Four for a record-tying 12th time under the guidance of Mike Krzyzewski.

13 GUARD

MATT JONES

Versatile Starter Comes up Big in Texas
By Leslie Gaber

With so much attention and praise heaped on senior leader Quinn Cook and the freshman trio of Tyus Jones, Jahlil Okafor and Justise Winslow, it is easy to overlook the contributions of the team's fifth starter — Matt Jones. The sophomore guard's spectacular performance in Sunday's win over Gonzaga made it impossible to ignore his impact on the Blue Devils.

"Matt gave us such a huge lift," said head coach Mike Krzyzewski after Duke dispatched the Zags to earn a trip to the Final Four in Indianapolis. "He's been that dirty-work guy, and for him to hit those four 3s, it was a big difference."

Jones finished the game with 16 points on 6-of-10 shooting, including 4-of-7 from three-point range, to go along with three rebounds and three steals. The timeliness of his scoring was impeccable as nearly every basket he made dealt a body blow to the Zags.

"I just tried to stay in the moment," Jones said. "All those shots that we hit were for the team. They were our shots."

Jones opened the contest by contributing on the offensive end immediately, scoring on a layup less than two minutes into the game to give Duke a 5-4 lead. Moments later, over a span of less than a minute, Jones would contribute on back-to-back trips down the floor, as he assisted on a Tyus Jones layup and then hit his first 3-pointer of the game on Duke's next possession to push the lead to eight points.

The timeliness of Jones' threes was unquestionable as he twice nailed a 3-point field goal when the game was tied. With the score knotted at 31-31, Jones drilled a three off of a Tyus Jones assist. With the game once again tied, this time at 38-38, Jones brought down a defensive rebound and hit a 3-pointer with the shot clock running down. His final trey of the game came when Gonzaga had cut Duke's lead to within three as the scoreboard read 45-42. Jones' 3-pointer gave Duke a six-point lead that Gonzaga was unable to overcome over the final 10 minutes of the game.

In the waning seconds, Jones had a key steal and his subsequent fast-break layup with 45 seconds left ended the last faint hopes of a Bulldogs' comeback.

The always humble Jones, who joined the Duke starting lineup in late February, passed off praise in the postgame press conference to his teammates.

Matt Jones finishes an easy layup after stealing the ball from Gonzaga's Kyle Wiltjer in the waning seconds of Duke's 66-52 win over the Bulldogs. Jones was named to the all-tournament team, hitting 4-of-7 attempts from beyond the arc on his way to 16 points in the contest. (Jon Gardiner/Duke Photography)

"Playing with such great players in the starting five, Marshall and Grayson and Amile as well, you tend to find open spots," Jones said. "Teams usually lose me in transition or the flow of offense. Luckily, I was able to hit a couple shots and help my team to the victory."

Jones also gave a subtle nod to his favorite high school postgame treat as the trip to Texas allowed him to enjoy Whataburger's No. 5 with fries and a drink. "I missed it so much," Jones said of the fast food meal.

Talented teammates, the confidence of Coach K and regular visits to Whataburger make any trip special. Punching a ticket to the Final Four in the process just causes that hometown fast food joint burger to taste that much better. ■

2

QUINN COOK

Senior Captain Relishes Final Four Opportunity
By Steve Wiseman • April 2, 2015

It was a few minutes after noon on Thursday when Quinn Cook looked around to soak in his environs inside Lucas Oil Stadium.

With Cook on a dais for an official Final Four press conference were Kentucky's Willie Cauley-Stein, Wisconsin's Frank Kaminsky and Michigan State's Travis Trice.

Both Cauley-Stein and Kaminsky have been named first-team All-Americans this season. Cook's own coach, Duke's Mike Krzyzewski, called Trice the best player in the NCAA Tournament so far.

Cook, though, didn't feel small. The Duke senior is finally on college basketball's biggest stage — the Final Four — and it's as great as he thought it would be.

"I'm like a kid in a candy store here," Cook said.

Cook knows too much about March's vast emotional spectrum. As a freshman, Cook was part of Duke's team that was bounced from the tournament by Lehigh.

Last season, when Cook was a junior, the Blue Devils lost to Mercer in the NCAA Tournament.

In between, the Blue Devils won three tournament games in 2013 to reach the Midwest Regional final. An 85-63 loss to Louisville prevented Duke from making that year's Final Four.

Quinn Cook looks to finish a layup as Robert Morris' Marquise Reed attempts to alter the shot in an NCAA Tournament second round meeting between the two teams in Charlotte, N.C. (Jon Gardiner/Duke Photography)

With Duke taking its place alongside Wisconsin, Kentucky and Michigan State in a star-studded Final Four field, Cook appreciates what it all means for he and the Blue Devils.

"I've had two early exits in the first rounds, losing to Louisville in the Elite 8, seeing those guys cut the nets down, celebrate, remembering that," Cook said. "It's a blessing to be here, especially with these three guys. These four historic programs here, it's a dream come true for myself."

While a productive player, Cook isn't a first-team, All-American or a potential Most Outstanding Player in the tournament. But his importance to this Duke team can't be overstated.

As the lone senior scholarship player and one of the team's captains, Cook has set a tone for the group on and off the court. On a team with two freshmen — Jahlil Okafor and Justise Winslow — projected to be selected among the first 10 picks in the NBA Draft come June and a third starting freshman, Tyus Jones, also a projected first-round pick, Cook has helped create a culture that hasn't divided the group along class lines.

"I do think that it helps them tremendously to have at least one upperclassman who is a key player, not just upperclassmen who are on the team," Krzyzewski said. "In this case, Quinn has helped these guys."

Michigan State coach Tom Izzo has similar feelings for Trice, his senior guard who is averaging 19.8 points per game in this year's tournament.

There's a good chance Trice and Cook, side-by-side at Thursday's press conference, will be guarding each other on Saturday night's game.

"I was telling Mike earlier," Izzo said Thursday, "Quinn Cook, for me, you just appreciate him because we got a chance, meaning not there every day, to watch a kid grow throughout the year. For Travis Trice for me, I got a chance to do it from the inside looking out."

In a sport where there's so much emphasis and attention paid to one-and-done freshmen like Okafor, Winslow or Kentucky's Karl-Anthony Towns, a guy like Cook has proven to make a big difference between a talented team and a championship team.

"I'm so thankful that Quinn has been there for me this year, to have a senior that I've been able to grow with, it's helped the team a lot," Krzyzewski said.

Cook will only get to play in one Final Four — this one — before his Duke career ends. The trials and tribulations of a four-year career as a whole, and this season's team in particular, have increased his appreciation.

"I'm blessed to be where I am on this team," Cook said, "because we've been through a lot this year, a lot on the court, off the court. We always have trust in each other. Coach never gave up hope and always encouraged us. I'm just blessed to be up here." ∎

Quinn Cook dials up a three against Gonzaga early in the contest to give Duke an eight-point lead. Cook knocked down 11 3-pointers and averaged 13.5 points per game in the NCAA Tournament. (Jon Gardiner/Duke Photography)

APRIL 4, 2015 • INDIANAPOLIS, INDIANA
DUKE 81, MICHIGAN STATE 61

RACK 'EM UP

Duke Rides Defense Past MSU to Title Game

By Steve Wiseman

Duke waited five years, and all the current Blue Devils their entire careers, to play in the Final Four.

Over the first few minutes of Saturday's NCAA Tournament semifinal against Michigan State, it appeared the Blue Devils were just happy to be there.

Coach Mike Krzyzewski, during the first timeout with his team down eight points, corrected that attitude.

"Coach does what he does. He gets their attention," Duke assistant coach Nate James said. "We were able to get back to what we were supposed to be doing."

With that, Michigan State's chances to win dwindled to nothing, and Duke forced its way into another national championship game appearance.

The Blue Devils erased that early deficit by clamping down defensively to open an 11-point halftime lead and roll to an 81-61 win over the Spartans.

The dramatic turnaround means Duke

(34-4) will play for the NCAA Tournament championship Monday night against Wisconsin. The Badgers upset previously unbeaten Kentucky 71-64 in the second semifinal Saturday night.

It's the third time Duke has reached the NCAA Tournament final in Indianapolis. The Blue Devils claimed national championships in 1991 and 2010 in Indiana's capital city.

"Being in a national championship game," Krzyzewski said, getting emotional, "it's crazy how lucky you are. This team deserved to be in it."

All season long, Krzyzewski has expressed his admiration — love is the term he's freely used — for his team that features three freshmen starters.

That love was likely waning when Michigan State hit five of its first seven shots, including four of four 3-pointers, to build a 14-6 lead.

"We were not guarding them the way we should have been," James said.

A classic, emphatic Krzyzewski message during a media timeout with 15:44 left in the first half changed that. Duke's players were sharper

Matt Jones attempts an acrobatic shot while avoiding the outstretched arm of Michigan State's Branden Dawson in Duke's Final Four meeting with the Spartans. Duke's defense forced Michigan State into 14 turnovers, which the Blue Devils scored 19 points off of throughout the game. (Jon Gardiner/Duke Photography)

on defense, and the Blue Devils mixed some zone defense with their man-to-man sets.

"We came out not as intense as we like to be," Duke freshman guard Tyus Jones said. "They hit their first four or five shots and a number of them were 3s. We were just giving them too many good looks. We weren't sticking to our game plan."

Michigan State (27-12) missed 17 of its next 20 shots over the rest of the first half as Duke took a 36-25 lead at intermission.

After that important early timeout, Duke scored seven points in a row as Michigan State went scoreless on its next six possessions.

"A couple of times," Duke senior guard Quinn Cook said, "I know myself, I tried to cheat on a ball screen. (Travis) Trice and (Denzel) Valentine make you pay. We got down early, but coach got on us. That last 36 minutes, I mean, we played one of our better games, just defensively, which led to great offense."

Trice scored a layup to temporarily keep the Spartans in front, but a basket and free throw from Duke freshman center Jahlil Okafor with 10:06 left in the half tied the score at 16. It also started another 7-0 Duke run. This one put the Blue Devils in front for good.

Duke's third 7-0 run of the half came after Branden Dawson rebounded his own miss to score for Michigan State with 6:01 left in the half.

That would be the Spartans' final field goal of the half.

"They did a good job of taking me away," said Valentine, who hit three 3-pointers over the game's first four minutes but only scored two points the rest of the half. "I got hot. They started denying me a little bit, started forcing me to take bad shots. Next thing you know, they had a lead."

That third 7-0 run allowed the Blue Devils to grab control of the game for good.

Duke scored the first six points of the second half,

Jahlil Okafor creates space on his way to the basket for two of his 18 points. (Jon Gardiner/ Duke Photography)

NOTABLE: Jahlil Okafor provided 18 points on the offensive end of the floor to become the first freshman in Duke history to record 34 double-digit scoring games in a season.

NOTABLE: Duke's offense remained strong throughout the second half of the game, with the Blue Devils not allowing the Spartans to pull any closer than 13 points.

After trailing 14-6 less than four minutes into the game, Duke's offense responded by going on a 23-6 run over the next 12 minutes.

part of a stretch where the Blue Devils made eight of their first 12 shots after halftime, to take a 54-34 lead with 13:30 to play.

Duke shot 52 percent, using their superior athleticism to drive past the Spartans for shots at the rim. The Blue Devils made just 2 of 10 3-pointers, missing all four of their second-half attempts from behind the arc.

But it didn't hold Duke back.

Freshman forward Justise Winslow continued his strong NCAA Tournament with 19 points for Duke. Okafor, Duke's first-team all-American, scored 18 points, and senior guard Quinn Cook scored 17.

Scoring 81 points without being successful behind the 3-point line was something Duke was prepared to execute.

"Outside shots weren't falling for us," Tyus Jones said. "But Jah was playing such a great game down low. Quinn was able to get to the basket. Matt (Jones) was able to drive. Same with Justise. Guys were really driving the ball well."

And that, along with renewed effort on defense, has the four-time national champion Blue Devils playing in the NCAA Tournament championship game for the 11th time in school history. ■

Grayson Allen drives and goes up strong for a layup while Michigan State's Branden Dawson contests the shot. Allen provided nine points and five rebounds in 17 minutes of action to serve as a perfect catalyst off the bench. (Jon Gardiner/Duke Photography)

NOTABLE: Duke asserted itself close to the rim against the Spartans posting a 42-26 advantage in points in the paint.

APRIL 6, 2015 • INDIANAPOLIS, INDIANA
DUKE 68, WISCONSIN 63

FRESHMEN FEVER

Jones, Allen Lead Duke to Fifth NCAA Title

By Steve Wiseman

The freshmen delivered all the points after halftime.

The entire team contributed the necessary defensive stops to erase Wisconsin's second-half lead.

With that, Duke thrived in its drive for five.

Freshman guard Tyus Jones scored 23 points — 19 in the second half. Another freshman, season-long, often-forgotten reserve Grayson Allen scored 16 points — 10 in the second half.

Down nine with 13 minutes to play, Duke displayed the poise of a team built of veterans, not freshmen, and defeated Wisconsin 68-63 in the NCAA Tournament championship game at Lucas Oil Stadium Monday night.

"My team had great grit and determination," said Duke coach Mike Krzyzewski, who has led the Blue Devils to five NCAA championships in his 35 years as their coach. "Our defense down the stretch was magnificent. We scored. I mean, I don't know how you can be any better than we were down the stretch. Great, great stuff. I'm proud of my team."

There's plenty to be proud of with a team that had only eight scholarship players in its rotation for the last two months of the season. Half of them were technically freshmen, but they never looked the part of scared teenagers.

With Wisconsin (36-4) and Duke (35-4) tied at 31-all at halftime, those four freshmen combined for all 37 Duke points over the final 20 minutes.

That included a 10-0 run that turned Wisconsin's 58-56 lead with 4:25 to play into a 66-58 Duke lead with 1:24 left.

Tyus Jones, named the Final Four's most outstanding player, hit 3-pointers to start and finish the run. All-American center Jahlil Okafor, whose title game production was limited by foul trouble, scored a pair of baskets inside in between Jones' 3-pointers.

"They're amazing," Duke senior guard Quinn Cook said of Duke's freshmen. "They're amazing. I mean, they make up half our team. There's four of them. They came so close, so

Tyus Jones releases a jumper over Wisconsin's Bronson Koenig in the national championship game in Indianapolis, Ind. Jones hit a pair of crucial threes late in the game to propel Duke to its fifth national championship (Jon Gardiner/Duke Photography)

Grayson Allen drives past Wisconsin's Duje Dukan during the national championship. Allen came off the bench to score 16 points, including eight straight points during a crucial second half comeback. (Jon Gardiner/Duke Photography)

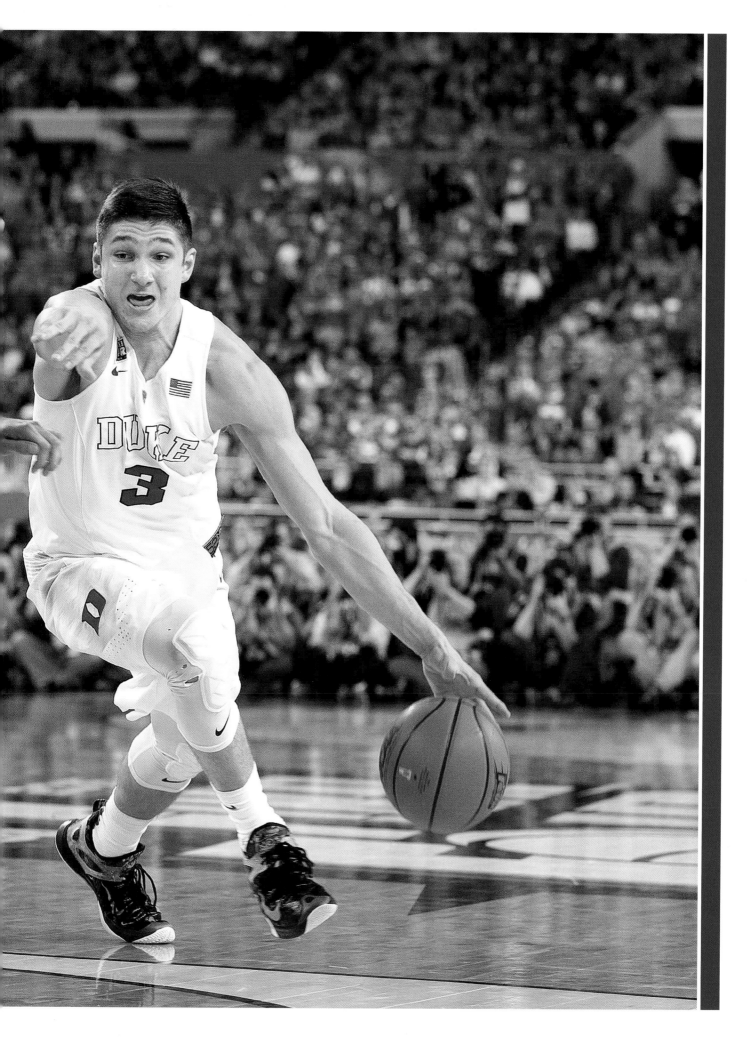

together and so humble. It was all about the team. All of them worked."

Wisconsin coach Bo Ryan, whose veteran team fell short of winning the school's first NCAA title since 1941, still believes his way of building a team is best despite the outcome.

"We don't do rent-a-player, you know what I mean?" Ryan said. "Try to take a fifth-year guy. That's okay. If other people do that, that's okay. I like trying to build from within. It's just the way I am."

Duke's Okafor, the first freshman to win ACC player of the year and the projected top pick in the NBA Draft if he comes out, scored 10 points in the title game. He played only 22 minutes due to his four fouls.

Freshman Justise Winslow, another projected lottery pick in the NBA Draft, also had four fouls. He scored 11 points and grabbed nine rebounds.

Allen, a 6-4 guard who is the only Duke freshman who didn't start a game this season, cranked out his points with a variety of impressive drives to the basket against the taller, older Badgers.

On the night the title was won, a new hero emerged.

"We've got a team," Winslow said. "We have great players, but at the end of the day we have a team. That's what makes this special. We have different guys that can step up. Guys are versatile. Guys can score. Guys can pass, rebound and defend. That's what makes us so tough. Guys don't care who is scoring. Guys just care that Duke is the national champion."

Duke's fifth national championship means Krzyzewski is now second only to UCLA's John Wooden (10) in all-time championship wins by a Division I men's coach. He's already tied Wooden with 12 Final Four appearances.

With 13:49 to play Monday night, it looked like Krzyzewski was in danger of losing a title game for

Tyus Jones celebrates one of his two 3-point field goals during the national championship game against Wisconsin. Jones was a perfect 7-of-7 from the free throw line, including two free throws in the final minute to clinch the win. (Jon Gardiner/ Duke Photography)

NOTABLE: Tyus Jones was named the Final Four Most Outstanding Player, becoming just the fourth freshman to claim the honor and the first Blue Devil to earn regional and Final Four MOP honors.

the fifth time.

Wisconsin, with national player of the year Frank Kaminsky on his way to scoring 21 points, had forged a 48-39 lead.

But, with Winslow and Okafor on the bench with three fouls each, Allen ignited an 11-3 Duke run.

Allen hit a 3-pointer before batting away a pass on the perimeter to force a Wisconsin turnover. With 12:10 left, he drove the lane to hit a layup and draw a foul from Sam Dekker. Allen's free throw left Duke down 48-45.

Nigel Hayes answered by hitting an open 3-pointer for Wisconsin.

But Allen aggressively drove the lane again, this time drawing a foul from Duje Dukan. Allen's free throws with 11:43 to play left Wisconsin up 51-47.

Okafor and Winslow were still on the bench when, after Hayes missed a layup, Tyus Jones hit a runner from eight feet and drew a foul.

Jones' free throw with 10:42 to play cut Wisconsin's lead to 51-50 as Okafor returned to the game.

Okafor had a chance to put Duke in front, but missed a contested shot in the lane.

Moments later, Kaminsky converted a spin move around Okafor and sank a basket as Okafor fouled him on the arm. Wisconsin led 54-50 when Okafor left the game with his fourth foul.

Duke didn't crumble, though.

Winslow sank two free throws and, after Wisconsin went three possessions without scoring, Tyus Jones' 17-foot jump shot with 7:01 left tied the score at 54.

With 5:30 left, Allen's driving layup gave Duke its first lead of the second half at 56-54.

Kaminsky tied it at 56 minutes later for Wisconsin.

After Dekker gave Wisconsin a 58-56 lead, Tyus Jones drilled a 3-pointer with 4:06 left for a 59-58 Duke lead.

Duke's backcourt of Quinn Cook (left) and Tyus Jones (right) share an emotional moment with head coach Mike Krzyzewski (center) as the realization of the national title sinks in. (Jon Gardiner/Duke Photography)

> **NOTABLE:** Duke's four freshmen, Grayson Allen (16), Tyus Jones (23), Jahlil Okafor (10) and Justise Winslow (11), combined to score 60 of the Blue Devils' 68 points, the most by a group of freshmen in a national championship game. The Blue Devil freshmen scored all 37 of the team's second half points.

That started a 10-0 Duke run that turned the game — and the NCAA championship — toward the Blue Devils.

Kaminsky, guarded by Jefferson on the block, missed with 3:35 left. Okafor scored for Duke for a 61-58 lead.

Okafor's block of Kaminsky's shot, and Cook's deflection of the ball away from Kaminsky, resulted in a shot-clock violation and turnover for Wisconsin.

Okafor rebounded a Winslow miss and scored with 2:11 left to put Duke up 63-58.

When Tyus Jones drilled a 3-pointer, he screamed in joy as Duke led 66-58 with 1:24 to play.

The championship was returning to Durham when, just a few minutes earlier, that outcome had been in doubt.

"We faced a lot of adversity this year," Jones said. "We've been in a number of different situations in games, late in the second half when we've had to overcome. Tonight was just another one. We knew we worked too hard all year to just lay down and say we're down nine and we'll hand them the national championship."

And so the Blue Devils grabbed it and took it for their own. ■

Members of the team stand on stage and watch the 2015 NCAA Tournament One Shining Moment video while donning their national championship apparel. (Jon Gardiner/Duke Photography)

NOTABLE: Tyus Jones scored 19 of his 23 points in the second half of the game, including 10 in the last 7:04 of the contest. He hit two key three-pointers in the final five minutes of the game to give Duke the lead and put the contest out of reach for the Badgers.

Captain Quinn Cook holds his piece of the net, and Duke history, high as he turns to friends and family in the stands. (Jon Gardiner/Duke Photography)

3

GUARD

GRAYSON ALLEN

Grayson's Anatomy: Unsung Freshman Stars in Title Game
By John McCann • April 7, 2015

Duke's freshmen this. Duke's freshmen that.

All season long, everything was about Duke's three freshmen.

Except there were four of them.

Grayson Allen didn't get all that much love.

"He's been overshadowed, you can say," Duke freshman Justise Winslow said. "But we always believed in him."

From the get-go, the talk was about the likely one-and-done seasons for chiseled Winslow, big Jahlil Okafor and Tyus Jones, who's on the smaller side but had a huge 23-point burst Monday night against Wisconsin to help the Blue Devils get their hands on the trophy that came with the school's fifth national championship in basketball.

Duke beat Wisconsin 68-63 Monday in Lucas Oil Stadium.

Now, while Jones was out there thriving, Winslow and Okafor were floundering on the bench in foul trouble, and the Badgers stormed out of the locker room for the second half acting like that big trophy was going back to Wisconsin.

"Grayson put us on his back," Duke coach Mike Krzyzewski said. "We went to him kind of exclusively because of his ability to drive and penetrate. And he did. He finished."

He finished with 16 points, depositing 10 of them during the final 20 minutes. Midway through the second half, Allen scored eight straight points in 59 seconds on a 3-pointer, a three-point play and two more free throws. The young man was putting in work.

Grayson Allen attempts a three during Duke's 90-60 win over Notre Dame in Cameron Indoor Stadium. (Jon Gardiner/Duke Photography)

NOTABLE: Grayson Allen scored 27 points, second-most by a freshman coming off the bench in Duke history, in a March 4 win over Wake Forest. He was 9-of-11 from the field, including 4-of-5 from 3-point range in the contest.

Duke's freshmen scored all 37 of the team's points in the second half.

Okafor, Winslow and Jones started every game they played for Duke. Allen never started and showed up for the national championship averaging 4.0 points and 8.9 minutes per game. Yet he bothered the Badgers for 21 minutes, leaving the court as Duke's No. 2 scorer for the evening.

"Well, Coach has told me all year to stay ready and practice," Allen said.

Allen earned a spot on the all-Final Four team. The kid played like he was making a case for his own one-and-done campaign.

"I saw them win 2010, that national championship against Butler. I've dreamed about being in this moment since then," Allen said. "Never thought it would actually come true. But for it to happen, it's amazing. I'm lost for words."

Jones got the votes that distinguished him as the most outstanding player of the Final Four. Allen shared a spot on the all-Final Four team with Winslow and Wisconsin's Sam Dekker and Frank Kaminsky, the Associated Press player of the year.

"We always knew the type of player he was and that his day would come," Winslow said. "He's athletic. You can go on YouTube and see the type of things he can do. But, I mean, we all know the type of player he

is. That's why it's great to see it happen, but this doesn't surprise us. He's been doing this all year in practice."

"There are practices when Quinn [Cook] lights it up and torches the net. Same thing for Grayson," Duke reserve center Marshall Plumlee said.

"In practice, he's being aggressive. He's being a dog. No one wants to guard him because he's being so aggressive," Winslow said about Allen. "He's a dog. Coach calls him [a butthole] in practice. That's what he was, [a butthole] on the court. Playing hard. Guys didn't want to guard him out there. You saw that. He kept getting to the basket and kept making big plays."

"I saw openings to drive," Allen said. "Quinn has been a great shooter for us all year. They were really staying on him and not helping off.

That was able to give us open lanes to attack the basket. I just wanted to stay aggressive and go up and try to draw a foul."

Allen got five cracks from the foul line and made every one of them.

"He hit his free throws," Krzyzewski said.

There's a character named Deebo in the *Friday* movie franchise. Deebo is a bully. Allen is Deebo, said Cook, who gave the rookie that nickname not long after they met.

"He always walks around mad, like he's trying to beat somebody up. That's why I called him Deebo," Cook said. "A little Deebo swagger."

To hear Allen tell it, a guy's got to have an edge about him if he's going to scrap every day in practice with dudes like Jones and Cook.

"We push each other in practice because we know that's what's going to make us better," Allen said. "So, I mean, that was big preparation for me to be in this moment." ∎

Grayson Allen elevates and throws down a dunk at the Greensboro Coliseum as N.C. State's BeeJay Anya watches. (Jon Gardiner/Duke Photography)

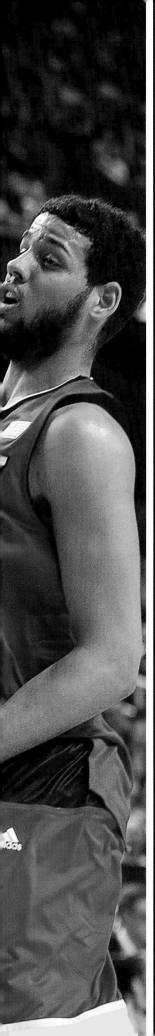

5 GUARD

TYUS JONES

Freshman Floor General Is Known for His Clutch Play
By Leslie Gaber

On a team that featured plenty of size and frontcourt talent, it was one of Duke's smaller players — six-foot guard Tyus Jones — who delivered some of the biggest performances when it mattered most.

Playing with senior captain Quinn Cook in the backcourt and surrounded by teammates who already knew what he was capable of, Jones wasted little time in stepping into his role. In just the third game of the season and the Blue Devils' first against a ranked opponent, he turned in 17 points, four assists, and zero turnovers in an 81-71 victory over Michigan State.

In Duke's first meeting with Wisconsin in December — which also marked the team's first road game against a ranked opponent — Jones again played a prominent role. The rookie helped spur a 6-0 Blue Devil run that pushed the margin to nine with three minutes left on the clock. Playing in front of numerous friends and family who made the trip from his hometown of Apple Valley, Minn., he totaled 22 points and four assists with just one turnover while leading Duke to 65 percent shooting on the day.

Displaying the poise and maturity of an older player, Jones continued to shine under pressure. He poured in 21 points against reigning national champion Connecticut before a pro-Huskies crowd at the Izod Center in the Meadowlands. In January, he logged back-to-back 22-point showings in wins over Pittsburgh and St. John's, the latter of which marked the 1,000th victory of head coach Mike Krzyzewski's career.

"He's good. You start out with that," Krzyzewski said of his young point guard. "One of the reasons we waited three years to get him is because I thought

Tyus Jones dishes a pass from underneath the basket during Duke's 77-53 win over N.C. State in the quarterfinal round of the ACC Tournament. Jones posted an eight-assist game in the victory. (Jon Gardiner/Duke Photography)

he had special qualities, not just special talents. It shows up in big games and big moments."

Jones and Cook teamed up to spark a furious Duke rally at No. 2 Virginia in early February, ending the Cavaliers' 21-game home winning streak with a 69-63 victory at John Paul Jones Arena. Both connected on key three-pointers late, helping the Blue Devils round out the game on a 16-5 run to knock off the previously undefeated Cavaliers.

If Jones hadn't already solidified his status as a clutch performer, his two games against Tobacco Road rival North Carolina certainly did. Duke let a 13-point lead get away in the February meeting in Cameron Indoor, and the Tar Heels capitalized, going up by 10 with less than four minutes to play in regulation. Jones tallied nine straight points in response, with his driving layup in the final minute tying up the game at 81. Despite a back-and-forth overtime period, the Blue Devils emerged victorious, 92-90.

"I'm just trying to make a play," Jones said afterward in the locker room. "My brothers believe in me, to have the ball in my hands, and that gives me all the confidence in the world, knowing that they have confidence in me. That's all I need is their confidence. I'm just trying to make a play and just being a competitor, hating to lose."

He proved clutch again when the rivalry was renewed in Chapel Hill less than a month later, scoring 17 of his 24 points in the second half to key an 84-77 Duke victory. After the Blue Devils overcame a poor shooting start, it was Jones who took over to help erase a seven-point deficit early in the second period. He drained a trey following a North Carolina turnover and, after another takeaway, found Cook for another dagger from deep.

In doing so, the freshman became the first Duke player to record at least 20 points and seven assists in each of his first two games against the Tar Heels.

Teammate Jahlil Okafor knew of Jones' potential from the beginning, as the two were famously recruited as a package deal by many college basketball powerhouses. Choosing Duke, they agreed, gave them the best chance to chase their dreams of a national title.

"It started off with basketball, with us wanting to win a national title," Okafor said to Jeff Eisenberg of Yahoo Sports. "He's a point guard, I'm a big man and we complemented each other really well when we were on the same team in practice. Then we also got extremely close off the floor, and he became like my brother. I've always said if you take basketball out of the equation, I'd still want to go to college with Tyus."

Jones' performance in the NCAA Tournament, then, came of little surprise. He averaged 13 points, 4.5 assists and 1.7 steals per game during Duke's run to the program's fifth title and shot 91.7 percent from the free throw line (22-of-24), sinking all seven of his attempts in the championship game. His late-game heroics were on display one final time against the Badgers, as he unleashed two treys inside the final five minutes to help the Blue Devils outscore Wisconsin by 14 points over the final 13 minutes of the game.

"He's going to get a lot better, but people have already seen him and know how he handles himself, especially in pressure situations and in the biggest games," Krzyzewski said.

For Jones, who most recently joined fellow freshmen Jahlil Okafor and Justice Winslow in declaring for the 2015 NBA Draft, taking this year's team as far as it could go was the goal from the start.

"I just wanted to be a part of a special team," he says. "I knew Grayson (Allen), Justise and Jah even before we got to campus. I just trusted Coach K and everyone on the staff with all my heart. I believed in everything that they told me. I just wanted to help, you know, contribute to such a special group. I wanted to go somewhere where I knew we would win." ∎

Tyus Jones shined under some of the brightest lights during the 2014-15 season, making big plays when the Blue Devils needed them the most. [Jon Gardiner/Duke Photography]

HOMECOMING FOR THE AGES!

By Keith Upchurch • April 7, 2015

Thunderous applause shook Cameron Indoor Stadium Tuesday as thousands of Duke fans welcomed back their all-time heroes — the men's basketball team and 2015 national champions.

"This has been my favorite year," head coach Mike Krzyzewski told the crowd. "My guys have been an absolute joy to coach."

Krzyzewski was joined on stage by his players, who defeated Wisconsin Monday night to win the NCAA Tournament for the fifth time in Duke's history and Coach K's tenure.

He called his team "outstanding" and said players had motivated themselves "for the most part."

"Our team has been a team of believers," Krzyzewski said, praising senior point guard Quinn Cook for helping provide the glue that kept the team solid. "He's been as good a leader as I've had in 35 years of coaching."

Cook, the lone senior non-walk-on in the program, thanked the fans, saying they made his last year at Duke "magical."

"You guys are the best," he said. "We couldn't have done it without your support."

Krzyzewski, who has led men's basketball at Duke since 1980, said: "There's nothing like the moment that you know you've won a national championship. And to be able to share it with all of you is terrific."

He said President Barack Obama phoned him Tuesday to congratulate the team's victory. He said Obama praised the players "not just for how they play basketball, but for how they represent their university."

Coach K said he wants to savor the win before talking about next season.

"What we try to do all year is enjoy the moment, and we're going to enjoy this moment," he said. "I hope you'll enjoy it with us."

The stadium was packed with people doing just that, including a family who drove to Durham from Florence, South Carolina, for the celebration.

Lisa Newell, 43, made the three-hour trip, as she has for Duke's four other national championships.

"I've been a Duke fan since I was 5," she said.

When Duke won Monday night, Newell said, she was "crying like a baby."

"It was just like I was out on the court with them," she said.

Duke junior Nicole Ryu, 21, said her school's win was like a dream come true.

"It was unreal," she said. "You don't believe it actually happened."

Ryu said the bonfire on the West Campus quad that followed the game was equally "incredible."

"The energy was unmatched anywhere," she said. "People's shirts actually got burned, but you think of it as a memento."

For Duke junior Jake Theios, the victory was life-changing.

"It was insane," he said. "People were crying, and my voice was so sore from screaming the whole time. I've never felt happier in my entire life." ∎

Duke celebrates its national championship with friends, family and fans in Cameron Indoor Stadium one day after earning the title. (Jon Gardiner/Duke Photography)

The Herald-Sun

TUESDAY, APRIL 7, 2015   HERALDSUN.COM $1.00

DUKE CAPTURES NCAA TITLE, 68-63, OVER WISCONSIN

DEVILS TAKE 5

8 PLAYERS IS ENOUGH • 13 LEAD CHANGES IN FIRST HALF • COACH K'S 1,018TH DIVISION I WIN

The Herald-Sun | Bernard Thomas

Duke's Tyus Jones reacts at the Blue Devils' victory over Wisconsin on Monday night, after they capture the school's fifth national championship.

Duke withstands explosive Badgers in second half for championship win

BY JOHN MCCANN
JMCCANN@HERALDSUN.COM; 919-419-6601

INDIANAPOLIS

The 13 lead changes in the first half didn't have a thing to do with whether these two No. 1 seeds in the NCAA Tournament wanted it.

The 31-31 halftime deadlock was a combination of Duke handling business in the paint and Wisconsin badgering the devil out of Coach Mike Krzyzewski's guys on the glass.

Wisconsin outdid Duke on the offensive backboards by an 8-2 margin in the first half. The Blue Devils needed to get a handle on that in the second half if they were going to bring home the big trophy from the Big Dance.

EXTRA, EXTRA: SPECIAL EDITION

The Herald-Sun's souvenir edition on Duke's championship is available at regular retail locations, from street vendors and at our office, 1530 N. Gregson St.

The Badgers exploded out of the locker room for the final 20 minutes of the season. Coach Bo Ryan's guys were starting to run away with the game. Krzyzewski needed a timeout to keep this one from getting out of hand.

Duke regrouped and won 68-63, delivering Krzyzewski's fifth national championship.

CAMERON GETS CRAZY

BY KATIE JANSEN
KJANSEN@HERALDSUN.COM;
919-419-6675

DURHAM — The students at the front of the line for the National Championship watch party at Cameron Indoor Stadium waited for more than an hour to see Duke face off against Wisconsin, but that was nothing compared to the weeks they'd spent sleeping in tents for other Duke basketball games throughout their college careers.

For this season's game versus Notre Dame, senior Chris Podracky said, they started lining up the night before the game to be ensured a seat.

The Herald-Sun | Alex Tricoli

Jack Grady, sophomore, center, cheers before watching the game broadcast at Cameron Indoor Stadium.

So arriving at Krzyzewskiville at 6:45 p.m. before the doors opened at 8 didn't seem like much of a sacrifice to

him and senior Jeremy Fischer — and it guaranteed them spots at the

SEE CRAZY/PAGE A2

INSIDE TODAY

LOCAL

Sidewalk support

Commissioners edging toward endorsement of project at Erwin and Randolph roads | A3

MUSLIM STUDENTS' DEATHS

Judge OKs death penalty bid for Hicks

BY KEITH UPCHURCH
KUPCHURCH@HERALDSUN.COM; 919-419-6612

DURHAM — A judge told prosecutors Monday they can legally seek the death penalty against a man accused of murdering three Muslim college students.

Durham County Superior Court Judge Orlando Hudson said prosecu-

tors had established two aggravating factors in the Feb. 10 gunshot deaths of the three victims — a legal requirement to seek capital punishment.

Durham County District Attorney Roger Echols said he will seek the death penalty against 46-year-old Craig Stephen Hicks of Chapel Hill.

Hicks has been charged with first-degree murder in the slayings of Deah Shaddy Barakat, 23; his wife, Yusor Mohammad Abu-Salha, 21; and her sister, Razan Mohammad Abu-Salha.

Their bullet-riddled bodies were

SEE HICKS/PAGE A2

CALL US
■ News:
919-419-6630
■ Advertising:
919-419-6700
■ Classifieds:
919-419-6910

DELIVERY QUESTION?
Circulation: 919-419-6900
SEE A NEWS ERROR?
Call our newsroom at 919-419-6678 or send an email to corrections@heraldsun.com

Copyright 2015,
Durham Herald Co. Inc.

WE ARE DURHAM

Business	A10	Obituaries	A4
Classifieds	B5-7	People	A12
Comics	B9	Sports	B1
Crossword	B8	Television	A12
Editorials	A11	World	A7

Weather

T-storms likely
high 73, low 62 | A12